SURVIVORS!

TRUE DEATH-DEFYING ESCAPES

by
Larry Verstraete

Design by Andrea Casault

Scholastic Canada Ltd.
Toronto New York London Auckland Sydney
Mexico City New Delhi Hong Kong Buenos Aires

Scholastic Canada Ltd.
175 Hillmount Road, Markham, Ontario L6C 1Z7, Canada

Scholastic Inc.
555 Broadway, New York, NY 10012, USA

Scholastic Australia Pty Limited
PO Box 579, Gosford, NSW 2250, Australia

Scholastic New Zealand Limited
Private Bag 94407, Greenmount, Auckland, New Zealand

Scholastic Ltd.
Villiers House, Clarendon Avenue, Leamington Spa,
Warwickshire CV32 5PR, UK

Cover photograph © Getty Images/Digital Vision
Design by Andrea Casault

National Library of Canada Cataloguing in Publication
Verstraete, Larry
Survivors! : true death-defying escapes / Larry Verstraete.
ISBN 0-439-98910-8
1. Survival after airplane accidents, natural disasters, etc.
2. Natural disasters—Anecdotes. I. Title.
GF86.V47 2003   904   C2002-904297-6

6 5 4 3 2 1   Printed in Canada   03 04 05 06 07

*For Faith, Janet, Judy and Lisa —
friends and fellow writers*

Many people came to my assistance throughout the writing of this book. To each one, I owe a debt of gratitude.

First and foremost, to the survivors themselves who lived these stories and whose experiences give us much to think about — thank you. In particular I would like to acknowledge the following people who spoke so frankly and openly in conversations with me: Jeffrey Bush, Christine Fram, Ed Glanz, Gerard Jensen, Nancy Kozlovic, Natalie McCarthy, Herbert Nishimoto, Angela Paulson, Kenneth Rutland, Jake and Lee Wieland, Jim Tarpley, and Joe, Tim and Teresa Spring.

Thank you, as well, to Larry Sorce and Warren Nishimoto, who were instrumental in providing leads and information, and to Bev Spencer, for her advice in the early stages of this book. I am also indebted to Barbara Hehner, for fastidiously confirming facts and finding additional details; to Joanne Richter, for locating and collecting just the right photographs; and to Sandra Bogart Johnston, Senior Editor at Scholastic Canada, for her sound judgment and expert guidance.

Other people have been helpful, too, often in subtle and less obvious, but equally important ways. To family and friends, thank you for your interest and encouragement. Thank you especially to those in Writer's Group — your friendship and trusted advice helped provide shape and substance for this book.

Above all, I would like to thank Jo, Stephen and Ashley, my special three, who not only listened, but gave me, as always, time and unbridled support.

TABLE OF CONTENTS

A note regarding this book:

The survivors in these true stories did their best, under the circumstances they faced at the time, to get themselves out of danger. The author has provided information from recognized sources to cover general situations in regard to surviving animal attacks, natural disasters, crashes, and so on. Any situation you might actually find yourself in might not be exactly the same as the ones described in the entries themselves, or in the Tips for Survival. Therefore, your best course of action is always to be prepared, and to consult expert advice.

The publisher and author disclaim any liability from any injury that might result from the use, proper or improper, of the information contained in *Survivors!* We do not guarantee that the information in the Tips for Survival is complete, safe or accurate, nor should it be considered a substitute for your good judgment and common sense.

INTRODUCTION

Danger lurks everywhere, it seems. Eighteen-year-old Angela Paulson felt its icy grip on an Ontario lake one winter night. Stanley Praimnath saw it coming as he stood at his office window one unforgettable September day. It flickered to life in young Ed Glanz's classroom, a fiery presence. It rumbled out of a dark forest, snarling and clawing at Bram Schaffer.

The truth is, danger is all around us. It rears its ugly head in the most unlikely places, at the most unexpected times. It comes in many guises, sudden and swift. Tornadoes and avalanches, fires and explosions, blizzards and animal attacks — whatever the shape or form, the danger is very real.

Often people lose their lives in these situations, but every so often someone survives and literally walks away. We marvel at their luck and applaud their bravery, but we also catch ourselves wondering: What would *we* do in such circumstances? Would we be as fortunate?

The people in this book faced danger and survived its test, escaping with their lives. These are their stories — stories of courage overcoming fear, of determination defeating hopelessness, of life conquering death. As we read them, maybe we can learn a thing or two about survival ourselves.

1

SWEPT AWAY

Water poured through every crevice and crack, filling the room in minutes. Mary Ann Gerlach looked for something, anything, that would keep her afloat in the worst hurricane on record.

Mary Ann Gerlach woke to the sound of the screaming wind. It howled like a demon, rattling the bedroom door and shaking the walls with such force that pictures crashed to the floor. In moments, water started gushing under the door and around its frame.

The bedroom door heaved and bucked like a wild bronco. Mary Ann and her husband, Fritz, pressed their shoulders against it, trying to hold back the rising water. It was no use. Water poured through every crevice and crack. Soon it started streaming in through the windows, too.

In about five minutes, the bed was floating halfway to the ceiling and the Gerlachs were struggling to stay alive in the worst hurricane ever to strike Mississippi.

Forecasters had warned that Hurricane Camille was on its way. But Mary Ann and Fritz didn't want to leave their apartment on the second floor of the Richelieu Apartments in Pass Christian, Mississippi. Like many other residents of the apartment block, they decided to wait out the storm. After all, they had survived other hurricanes. They could ride out this one, too.

It was a deadly mistake. For days the storm had been brewing in the Caribbean, swirling, whirling and gathering strength. On August 15, 1969, it pounded Cuba, killing three people. Then Camille picked up speed. By the next day, it had grown into a monster — a Category 5 storm, the most powerful possible. Churning like an out-of-control top, Camille weaved across the Gulf of Mexico. Just before reaching land on August 17, it veered sharply, shifted direction and aimed for the city of Pass Christian.

The Richelieu Apartments before Hurricane Camille hit

Late that night Hurricane Camille hit the Richelieu Apartments head on. It ripped off shingles and eavestroughs, and hurled debris like a knife-thrower gone berserk. Worse than the wind and rain, though, was the storm surge — the wall of water that the hurricane brought with it. Like a giant vacuum cleaner, the swirling winds of the hurricane had sucked up sea water, creating a bulge of water two storeys high. When the hurricane reached land, the bulge did too. It came crashing down upon the Richelieu Apartments with shattering force. In minutes the building was flooded and threatening to collapse.

With water rising past her neck and the building shuddering around her, Mary Ann looked for something to keep her afloat. She found a sofa cushion drifting past and latched onto it. Above the howling wind, she heard popping and snapping, the sounds of the apartment being torn apart. I've got to get out, Mary Ann thought. She thrashed through the water, kicking herself free of wires and other debris, and swam out the second-storey bedroom window. Once outside, she looked back. It was dark, but she could see Fritz bobbing in the water. Then the entire apartment complex swayed and collapsed. Fritz disappeared in the ruin.

The wall of water swept the wreckage far inland, carrying Mary Ann with it. Although she kicked and fought, the current was too strong for her to resist. Waves lashed at her, forcing her to choke down great mouthfuls of sea water. She was tossed against buildings and hammered with debris. In no time, she was bloody from head to foot, struck by boards and scratched by exposed nails.

The surge carried Mary Ann above power poles and over houses. She could feel the current sucking at her body, dragging it down. She tightened her grip on the cushion. It's the only thing keeping me alive, she thought. Suddenly a wave battered her, ripping the cushion from her hands. She floundered and started to sink. Desperately, she reached out for something — anything — that floated by. She clutched a tree branch for a while. When that was torn from her hands, she found furniture and pieces of wood to keep her afloat.

The Richelieu Apartments lie flattened after the hurricane struck

As the fierce winds and rushing waters carried her farther away, Mary Ann began to tire. Her muscles ached and she knew she couldn't last much longer. She needed to get out of the water, to find something that would give her protection. When she drifted past a tree, she grabbed hold of one of the branches and clawed her way closer to the trunk. While the storm raged around her, she hugged the tree with all her might.

After half an hour, the storm surge retreated, sucking huge amounts of wreckage back into the sea. Mary Ann watched as a parade of furniture, cars and even entire houses floated past her. Her mind wandered and she thought of Fritz. Once again she saw him bobbing in the water, the apartment crashing down upon him. She hoped he was alive, but somehow, deep inside, she knew he wasn't. Drenched, shivering and covered with blood, Mary Ann hung onto the tree throughout the long, lonely night.

Rescuers found her the next morning, about twelve hours after she had been swept away. The storm had carried her almost 9 kilometres from the Richelieu Apartments. She was taken to a hospital, where she spent three weeks recovering from her wounds.

Although badly injured, Mary Ann Gerlach was also incredibly lucky. Of the twenty-four people who had stayed behind in the Richelieu Apartments, she was one of the few to survive Hurricane Camille.

Surviving a Hurricane

With the help of satellites and weather instruments, today's forecasters can track a hurricane's path with great accuracy. That usually gives people who live in the hurricane's path sufficient time to get themselves and their homes ready. Follow these survival tips from FEMA — the U.S. Federal Emergency Management Agency — and you, too, may survive if a hurricane ever strikes.

TIPS FOR SURVIVAL

• Plan an evacuation route. Then, if you are told to evacuate, you will already have an escape route worked out.

• Board up windows; anchor objects that might blow away, or bring them indoors. If you are in a storm-surge zone, elevate furniture on the ground floor or move it to an upper floor.

• During a hurricane watch, stay inside away from windows, skylights and glass doors, as flying shards of glass can be deadly. Avoid elevators, too. If the power goes out, you could be trapped inside.

• Stay tuned. If conditions worsen, a hurricane watch might be upgraded to a hurricane warning, and an evacuation order might be issued. Listen to radio and television updates in case the storm changes direction or becomes more severe.

EXPLOSION ON GALERAS

Stanley Williams bolted down the mountain, rocks whizzing past him and hot lava bombs splattering around his feet. The volcano had erupted, and he was in a race for his life.

Stanley Williams doesn't have to search far for memories of January 14, 1993. His head sometimes still rings with pain from the baseball-sized rock that crushed his skull, driving bone fragments into his brain. His legs are mottled and scarred from skin grafts and plastic surgery. He wears a hearing aid, and occasionally he has seizures. When he closes his eyes, he can see the faces of some of the nine people who died that day. They still wear the surprised and horrified looks he will never forget.

Galeras was a restless mountain in Colombia, a volcano with unpredictable patterns of activity. For decades it had been dormant. Then in 1989, Galeras erupted in sudden fury, spewing ash and rock into the sky, and raining it upon the city of Pasto in the valley below. Over the next three years it erupted several more times. Then there was a pause, a period of calm, as Galeras grew strangely quiet.

The lull in activity seemed to be the perfect opportunity to take a closer look. In early 1993, scientists from around the world gathered in Pasto, all anxious to study the mountain. With new-found information, they hoped to develop a warning system to predict future eruptions.

Stanley Williams, a volcanologist, headed a team of thirteen scientists. The morning of January 14, they travelled up the mountain in a convoy of jeeps. Lugging backpacks and sensitive equipment, they hiked across the steaming rubble to the crater rim. Once there, José Arlés Zapata, a Colombian chemist, radioed the observatory in Pasto. Galeras was still, he was told by seismologists. There was no sign of activity; no hint of a seismic blip; no twitches or rumbles inside the volcano. It was safe to go ahead.

The scientists split into smaller groups, each set to gather its own specific information. Some, like Igor Menyaliov and Nestor García, sampled gases in and around the crater. Others, like Geoff Brown, checked gravity levels around the rim. Still others took temperature readings or measured lava levels.

Seismologists in Pasto kept in touch with José periodically, issuing the latest reports on the volcano's activity. Because of José's position inside the caldera — the depression at the top of the volcano — shielded by rocks on all sides, radio signals were weak and scattered. To be heard, a scientist from another team farther away had to intercept the messages, and act as a relay between José and the observatory. Communication was sketchy and slow.

At one point, the observatory reported small squiggles appearing on the seismographs. A while later, it reported that the waves had disappeared. What was happening? Even highly trained scientists could not agree on what the signals meant.

Just after 1 p.m, after more than three hours on the mountain, the team prepared to leave. As the scientists gathered their equipment and began the slow trek back, a shower of rocks broke off the crater wall and thundered down the slope. Galeras was awakening.

Stanley shouted to the others, then turned to run. From the corner of his eye he caught a fleeting glimpse of Igor and Nestor as they scrambled to get out of the crater. Their faces wore stunned, surprised looks, looks of disbelief and fear. He spotted Geoff across the rim. Stanley waved and motioned to him to run for his life while there was still a chance.

The mountain shook and swayed. All at once there was an ear-splitting boom and Galeras exploded. Rocks whizzed by Stanley. Hot lava bombs splattered around his feet, and the ground quivered like jelly. Stanley bolted down the mountain. His only thought was of putting distance between Galeras and himself.

He was partway down the slope when the first rock struck him. It plowed into his head, cracked open his skull and threw him off course. He staggered, stumbled a step or two, then collapsed. He was vaguely aware that he was hurt, that here in the open he was a waiting target, and that he should get up and run. Somehow, though, his feet refused to obey the commands screaming in his head.

He looked to the side and saw a patch of yellow. It was José Arlés Zapata, his body twisted and crumpled, his head covered in blood. Not far away, Stanley spotted three other bodies thrown against the dark rock. Three more dead.

Stanley stumbled to his feet. His clothing was on fire, but running seemed more important than putting out the flames. He weaved through the obstacle course of hot rocks and steaming vents. A few metres along, a wave of rocks caught him from behind, snapping his legs like twigs, throwing him to the ground again. Beneath his smouldering pants, Stanley spotted white bone poking through his left leg. His right foot hung from his leg by threads of skin and muscle.

Other scientists who had survived the onslaught were on the run, too. They scrambled along the slippery slope, with rocks the size of footballs raining from the sky, and choking, sulphurous fumes filling their lungs.

"My leg is broken!" Stanley was yelling. "My leg is broken. It's severed!"

But the barrage of rocks made it impossible to reach him. He was alone, surrounded by destruction. Then some deep instinct took hold of Stanley. An inner voice told him to push aside the pain, to get up and hide. He tried. Painfully he dragged himself behind a boulder.

The mountain shook and roared. Clouds of ash rose into the sky, blotting out the sun, turning day into night. After about fifteen minutes it began to rain. The drops mixed with the ash, forming a thick muddy paste. Huddled against the rock, too injured to move, Stanley could only hope for rescue. Stay alert, he told himself. Stay awake.

An erupting volcano spewing red-hot lava

In time, the quaking stopped. Ignoring the possibility of another eruption, a handful of scientists farther away scurried up the slope. It seemed impossible that anyone so close to the crater could have survived the barrage of rock and lava, but they searched for survivors anyway. That much they owed their colleagues. Eventually they found Stanley, still crouched behind the rock, one of the lucky few to be spared by Galeras.

Stanley was severely injured. His jaw and nose were broken, and his skull was crushed.

The force of impact blasted small bones through his eardrums, destroying his hearing. His right foot was mangled and barely attached to his leg. He had deep burns over his ears, neck and legs.

Over the next two years Stanley endured seventeen operations. Doctors cut and pasted him together, grafting new skin to replace the old, reattaching his foot, repairing his crumpled body and ailing mind as best they could. Recovery was slow and painful, with months of therapy and rehabilitation. On his worst days, Stanley almost wished Galeras had finished the job it began.

———

Stanley Williams has come a long way since the accident. His wounds have healed, and the burn marks have faded. He can walk without a limp now, thanks to the gifted surgeons who worked on him. But the deepest scars are not the physical ones; they're mental and emotional. His mind is not as sharp as it once was. He mixes up words and numbers, forgets things and has trouble reasoning. Sometimes he has seizures, a result of the brain injuries he received.

Stanley has co-authored a book about his experiences, but his account is steeped in controversy. Some of the others who survived Galeras dispute his recollection of events, and hold him responsible in part for the tragedy. They claim he ignored safety procedures, downplayed early signs of activity, and spent too much time in the volcano, putting everyone on his team in jeopardy.

These charges notwithstanding, even his harshest critics cannot dispute that Stanley Williams has made a remarkable recovery. He has even been back to the mountain that almost killed him. Six years after the incident he returned to Galeras, walked its slopes and stared into its crater. It was part of the healing process — confronting the enemy once again.

INFERNO!

A blast of wind screamed through the tent, and a wall of flame roared up the slope, trapping the Hedges family in a deadly fire.

For the tenth time that hot August night, sixteen-year-old Kathleen Hedges reminded herself that there was no reason to worry. Her father, Pat, was captain of the fire department in Miles City, Montana. If anyone knew fires, it was her dad, and he had told Kathleen that the orange glow on the horizon was too far away to be of concern. After all, the wildfire had been burning steadily for weeks already, and it was still at least 16 kilometres away.

Kathleen and her fifteen-year-old brother, Keith, had spent the day hiking with their father and Misty, the family dog, along Horseshoe Canyon, a rugged area near Wyoming's Yellowstone National Park. That evening they pitched their tent on a ridge high above a creek. Like her dad and brother, Kathleen was bone-weary and her body craved rest. But her mind was alive with worry. While the others slept, she kept watch.

Suddenly, she froze. Had the distant glow just moved closer? The fire seemed brighter and taller than before.

"Dad," she called into the dark, "I see flames."

Her father sat up, sleep banished in an instant. Impossible, he thought. The fire's too far away. At almost the same moment, flames shot into the air from a ridge 450 metres below their camp. A wave of heat hit, then seconds later a blast of wind screamed through the tent. A wall of fire roared up the slope, shooting sparks into the air and turning the quiet woods into an inferno.

A firestorm! Somehow the simmering wildfire had turned ugly, transforming itself into a whirlwind of superheated air and flames with a life of its own. The deadly fire was charging through the forest, leaping ahead of itself, gobbling up trees at an alarming rate.

Pat Hedges's mind raced. He weighed the options, gauging them against his years of firefighting experience. To stay meant certain death, that much was obvious. To run, to escape through the thick brush hoping to beat the rush of flames — that was impossible. He knew that there was no way to outrun a firestorm. It moved too fast. Already the wind was whipping the air into a frenzy, filling the sky with burning embers, torching trees all around them.

There were only two choices, really. Scramble up the slope away from the fire and try to climb above the tree line. Or head *toward* the fire and the icy waters of the creek 45 metres below.

Climbing uphill to escape the fire would be hopeless, Pat decided. The trail up the slope was unfamiliar to him. Besides, they would have to climb more than a kilometre to get beyond the trees. They'd never make it. The fire would be upon them long before they reached safety.

The creek offered better chances. If they could reach it ahead of the fire, if they could lie in its cold waters as the fire closed over them, if . . .

"Quick. Grab your sleeping bags," Pat yelled. "We're going to the creek."

They stumbled down the hill, Kathleen clutching Misty and holding her tight. The smoke was thick, and they could barely see the ground, let alone each other. Above the roar of the fire, though, they could hear the faint sounds of bubbling water. The creek was just ahead, somewhere.

They stumbled over rocks, tripping on roots, slipping and sliding down the slope. Finally, their feet tasted cool wetness. The creek at last. But the water was only ankle deep at this spot — too shallow to lie in, certainly not deep enough to save their lives. They made their way downstream until they reached a rotten log that had fallen across the creek. Here the water was more than 30 centimetres deep.

"Lie down in the water," Pat said. "Soak your sleeping bags and pull them over you. Stay covered."

They settled in the creek and held hands as Pat offered a

quiet prayer. They needed a miracle now. The fire was just moments away.

Kathleen felt Misty squirm in her arms. She tried to calm the dog, but suddenly Misty broke free. Kathleen leaped to her feet. "Misty!" she yelled. But there was no answer, only a blast of wind, a blaze of heat and the thunder of trees crashing around them. Kathleen settled back down in the icy water. There was nothing else she could do.

Lying in the cold wet, Pat remembered something. Their backpacks! In the scramble to get to the creek, everything but their sleeping bags had been left behind. Without the backpacks, they had nothing — no food, no bandages, nothing. If he and his kids survived the firestorm, they would need to hike out of the charred forest. The supplies spelled the difference between life and death.

"Wait here," Pat said as he ran back up the slope. "I'm going for the backpacks."

Kathleen and Keith huddled in the stream. Misty had vanished. Now their father had gone, too. They were alone; the fire

would soon be upon them. Their lives depended on a few centimetres of water in a shallow creek, water so cold that their fingers were growing numb despite the stifling hot air around them.

Suddenly, they heard splashing nearby. It was their dad,
returning with three scorched backpacks. Then, they heard
another sound — a yelp, faint but clear. Misty! The dog was
alive after all. Pat whistled, and Misty charged from the flaming underbrush. Pat pulled the dog into the water and used his
belt as a makeshift leash to hold her close.

"Heads down," Pat yelled. "Try to keep your sleeping bags
wet."

A blanket of flame swept over the creek, lighting up trees
like giant candles. Sparks rained from the sky. Rocks sizzled
and popped from the heat. The wind screamed, and choking
smoke filled their lungs. A flying ember ignited one end of the
log that protected them. Kathleen quickly scooped up water
with her hands to put it out.

The fire seemed to rage forever. Then, suddenly, the howling stopped and the fire moved on up the mountain. It was
over. The cold water had numbed their limbs, and they shivered uncontrollably. Their concern was no longer the fire. It
was hypothermia.

"Out of the creek," Pat ordered.

They climbed out, jackets over their mouths to filter the
choking smoke. The forest was a charred wreck, a twisted
mass of smouldering stumps and thick smoke. Here and there,
spot fires licked the few trees still standing. The ground was
hot and covered with a layer of poisonous fumes. The Hedges
family would have to wait until the heat subsided and the haze
lifted before hiking out.

Beside a smoking log the three snuggled together, keeping
each other warm throughout the night. In the morning they
started the long trek back, through the blackened forest to
safety and home.

———

August 20, 1988, has been called Black Saturday. It was a day
of disaster for the Yellowstone region. That day, fire went on a

rampage, turning rich green forest into a charred wasteland, and leaving at least one family with lives that would never be quite the same again.

Surviving a Wildfire

Wildfires spread quickly, moving at incredible speeds as they ignite forests, brush and grasslands. You cannot outrun a wildfire, but you might be able to outsmart the deadly enemy:

TIPS FOR SURVIVAL

• Take refuge in a pond or river.

• Crouch low and keep wet. Cover your head and upper body with wet clothing if possible.

• Breathe the air closest to the ground through a wet cloth. This might help you avoid inhaling smoke or scorching your lungs.

• If there is no water around, find shelter in a cleared area or among an outcropping of rocks.

17

ADRIFT

The wave stormed the beach, collapsing on children, swallowing cottages and uprooting trees. As it swept higher, Herbert Nishimoto knew he had but one choice: to run for his life.

It has been more than fifty years since the giant wave changed Herbert Nishimoto's life, but the memory of April 1, 1946, stands tall and clear, as fresh as yesterday. It's one of those things that's hard to forget, even if you try.

Herbert was a lanky sixteen-year-old then, athletic and strong. He lived near Hilo, a fishing village on the east side of Hawaii's Big Island. That weekend there had been a picnic at Laupahoehoe School, and Herbert had spent the night in one of the school cottages near the beach.

Just before seven o'clock that Monday morning, Herbert awoke to the cries of Daniel Akiona, another student who lived nearby. "Herbert! Tidal wave! Tidal wave!"

Herbert pulled on his jeans and ran from the cottage to join others who had already gathered outside. He spotted a large wave — a tsunami — swelling out of the ocean. It towered above the others, and grew taller as it swept inland. The wave thundered onto the beach, and for a moment the bay was filled with water.

There was a lull, then the wave rolled back, and for several minutes revealed an eerie sight. It was as if a giant hand had reached down, pulled a plug and drained the bay. The blanket of water was peeled away, exposing the reef that stood guard over the harbour. Spotted eels squirmed out of crevices in the reef, and fish flopped in the sand along the beach. Despite the early hour, the unusual sight drew curious children, making their way to school, down to the bay. The ocean was doing very strange things, and they wanted a closer look.

A few minutes later there was a second wave even larger

than the first. It crashed upon the sand, ripping apart an old canoe house before climbing higher. With Daniel at his side, Herbert ran uphill toward the Akiona house.

A third wave rose and crested. This was a monster, higher and stronger than the others. The children close to shore panicked. They raced for higher ground, scrambling up the wet rocks, slipping here and falling there. One girl climbed a stone wall near the school.

The wave stormed the beach, collapsing on children, uprooting coconut trees and swallowing cottages whole. Herbert saw the girl on the stone wall disappear and, for a brief moment, he considered trying to save her. But the wave swept higher and Herbert knew he could do nothing for the girl. The only thing he could do was run for his life.

Herbert Nishimoto as an adult

He could hear the roar of the wave as it clipped his heels, the shifting of rocks and boulders. He climbed the porch railing around the Akiona house, but before he could make it over he felt the building shudder. It tilted crazily, then collapsed, a jumble of broken lumber. Then Herbert was yanked underwater, tossed and pounded by a force impossible to resist.

"I was tumbling, so I held my hands over my head and I tried to go out feet first because I didn't want my head to hit on the rock." Herbert remembers. "I looked back and I saw the principal's car being sucked out to sea."

The wave retreated, pulling Herbert into the ocean. It was like being in a giant washing machine. Logs, rocks, bits and pieces of homes, and Herbert, all being churned and ground together. When the wave finally released its hold, Herbert found himself on a rock near the reef. Daniel was nowhere to be seen.

Another wave was rising in the distance. Herbert tried to tear off his blue jeans, which were waterlogged and weighing him down. The jeans were tight around the ankle, and he managed to slip only one trouser leg off before the wave hit. He dove under the wave, anxious to escape the deadly rocks. The heavy pants trailed behind him, snagging on the reef and battering him against it as he was tossed back and forth. Finally, the wave caught him and dragged him out to sea. When he finally surfaced he was far from shore and drifting steadily farther.

Herbert was surrounded by debris. Boards, a mattress, entire walls and floors — reminders of lives now gone — littered the ocean. Herbert chased a duck off a floating log and hauled himself onto it. The log had a long cord attached to it. Herbert used it to tie the log to another, then he dragged boards out of the water and piled them on top. Using an old axe handle as a hammer, he pounded protruding nails into the

A tsunami can strike with deadly force

logs to hold together his makeshift raft.

A jar of shortening floated past, and Herbert fished it out of the sea. He smeared the greasy stuff over his body, hoping it would protect his skin from the sun and salt water. He found an old apple, too. He gobbled it down — core, seeds and all.

Herbert noticed that the duck had disappeared. He could see sharks in the water, hungrily searching for food, and he wondered if the duck had become their breakfast. He poked one of the sharks with the axe handle to chase it away. "I got scared," he says, "so I started putting lumber under me, even with the nails poking my stomach and feet, trying to keep afloat." He had to stay out of the water at all costs.

The water was still turbulent, and Herbert clutched the flimsy raft, determined to hang on. For hours he drifted on the rolling waves, alone in the vast ocean, watching the shoreline rapidly disappear from view. Every time he encountered more debris, he scooped it out of the water, adding useful pieces to his raft to make it sturdier and larger.

Around midmorning, he spotted two other boys floundering among the waves. One, fifteen-year-old Takashi Takemoto, floated on a door. The other, fourteen-year-old Asao Kuniyuki, rode a 190-litre oil can. Herbert edged the raft toward them, and helped them aboard. The two boys were relieved, but exhausted. In no time they were asleep.

Herbert tried paddling the raft, but it was too awkward to move and he was too tired to keep trying. The three boys were at the mercy of ocean currents now. Soon they were more than a kilometre away from shore, and land was just a hazy slit along the horizon.

That afternoon they heard the buzz of a plane. The pilot circled over them and dropped a bundle into the water. Herbert dove into the choppy ocean to retrieve it — an inflatable rubber raft, complete with aluminum paddles, fishing gear, a compass and flashers for signalling. He pulled the plug to inflate the raft, and the three boys scrambled aboard. The rubber raft was safer and more comfortable than their makeshift log one.

The three boys cling to life on their raft

The pilot had spotted them. Surely he'll return, Herbert thought. But the afternoon wore on and darkness soon fell, dashing his hopes for a quick rescue. He slept fitfully, waking often to keep watch. He could see lights in the distance. Civilization cannot be far away, he told himself.

The next morning the sun rose bright and hot. The boys were still far from shore, but they could feel the tug of the tide and knew that it was slowly dragging them closer to land. Features along the shoreline were growing more visible. Herbert could make out trees and buildings.

Around 11 a.m. they spotted a seaplane. A wavering dot in the distance, it was too far away for the pilot to even notice the three boys and their raft. The pilot doesn't even know we're here, Herbert thought. He grabbed the flashers to signal. The pilot seemed to see them, and for a brief moment their hopes soared. The plane circled over them . . . then, unbelievably, headed back to sea.

The circling plane attracted attention on land, though. A

schoolgirl saw the raft and called to plantation workers who were on their lunch break. Two workers dove into the water and swam to the boys. They dragged the raft back to shore.

Sunburned and exhausted, battered and bruised, Herbert and the others nevertheless beat the odds. They had been at sea for twenty-seven hours, drifted more than 80 kilometres, and survived one of the most devastating tsunamis ever to strike Hawaii.

———

Herbert Nishimoto says that, even during the worst of his ordeal, he somehow knew he would pull through. "It's a feeling you have, you know, like when you see a cowboy movie — the good guy is not going to die. I got that feeling . . . I had that confidence. I was not scared anymore."

Others were not so lucky. A total of 159 people were killed, most of them around Hilo. Of the dead, twenty-four students and four teachers were from Laupahoehoe School. Daniel Akiona was one of them. His body was never found. In a strange twist of fate, the seaplane that had circled over the boys returned to sea to save Daniel's mother, who had survived by floating on a door.

BURIED ALIVE

Avalanches tore down Grouse Mountain, ripping two hikers off the trail and burying them under a wall of snow. Ken Rutland was their only hope for survival.

Ken Rutland left his home in North Vancouver around noon on January 27, 1999. He dressed in warm layers and stuffed extra clothing in his backpack. In the city it was windy, wet and cold. On Grouse Mountain, Ken knew, temperatures would be even lower. At higher altitudes, rain could turn to sleet at a moment's notice.

Grouse Mountain lies just north of Vancouver, B.C., a dark hump of forest crisscrossed by a rugged trail known as the Grouse Grind. It's a popular place for hikers, and Ken, a fit thirty-five-year-old, was eager for the challenge.

Partway up the Grouse Grind, Ken met two men who seemed to be distressed. One of them had a cell phone and was calling for help. "There's been an avalanche!" they said. "Our friend's missing."

Ken calmed the two men as best he could, and headed down the trail to look for their friend. But on the way, he heard a soft moan. The sound came from a gully awash with fresh snow. There Ken found a man, his body wrapped around a tree, his legs buried deep in the snow. His face was pointed downhill at a steep angle and he clutched a branch as if his life depended on it.

Ken worked his way around the edge of the gully until he was beside the man, who said he was Masoud Shekarchi, another hiker. "My legs are broken," Masoud moaned. Ken dug around the man, trying to unearth him, but each move seemed to increase Masoud's pain. Then Ken saw a socked foot sticking out of the snow metres away. Oh my God, he thought. No wonder. His leg's been ripped off.

Almost immediately Ken realized his mistake. It wasn't

Masoud's leg. It belonged to another man buried deep in the snow. Quickly Ken scooped the snow away with his hands, knowing that time was critical. Victims of avalanches often suffocate to death within minutes, and Ken had no way of knowing how long this person had been buried. He dug through wet layers, clearing away the snow from the man's face. Then he checked for a pulse. Nothing. I'm too late, he thought.

Suddenly Ken felt a brief but definite beat, and for a moment he relaxed. The man, Karim Bhatia, drew a deep breath and opened his eyes. The force of the avalanche had bounced him down the gully, smashing him into trees and rocks, and ripping off his boots before covering him with smothering snow. Ken dug Karim out of his snowy grave, then assessed the situation. Other hikers knew of their where-abouts. Rescue teams were probably already on their way up the mountain. Keep them safe and warm, Ken told himself. That's the best you can do.

He searched his backpack, finding sweatpants, a neck tube and other spare pieces of clothing. He wrapped them around Karim, hoping to stem the icy cold filtering through his body. Then he carved a shelf out of snow, and hauled Karim over to it. He tried digging out Masoud, too, but the man cried out in agony whenever Ken touched him. Ken left Masoud where he was and did his best to clear the snow away from around him.

All at once Ken heard a chilling sound. On the still moun-tain, where echoes multiply, he heard the distant *whoosh* of air, the whisper of rushing snow. Avalanche! Before he could act, it was upon them.

Fortunately the snow cover wasn't heavy — barely 30 cen-timetres — and Ken was able to dig the men out again. But the second avalanche served as a warning. Conditions on the moun-tain were treacherous. There had been a lot of snow in the previ-ous days, and it had collected in fragile layers on the steep slope. An unexpected gust of wind, a faint tremor or sudden sound — any of these might release an even greater wave of snow.

Minutes later Ken's worst fears were realized. He heard a deep rumble far up the gully, and barely had enough time to brace himself before a wall of snow crashed over them. Karim was protected by the snow shelf, but Masoud was out in the open. The thundering snow caught him, sweeping him away. Ken reacted quickly. As Masoud flew past, Ken grabbed him just in time.

The third avalanche left both Karim and Masoud partially buried. Ken dug deeper into the snow, creating a safer and more sheltered shelf farther up the slope. He dragged Karim to it, then went back for Masoud. Just then, yet another avalanche tore down the mountain. Once again Ken braced himself for the onslaught. This one was worse than the others. It buried Karim up to his shoulders, and Ken up to his waist. But now there was no sign of Masoud. He was gone, lost under the snow.

Ken scanned the slope, looking for a sign. He had only a few minutes to find the man. Where was he? Then Ken noticed two fingers poking through the snow cover. He scooped the snow away as fast as he could, quickly exposing Masoud's head and shoulders, allowing the man to breathe again. Knowing that the avalanche would bury him, Masoud had done the only thing he could — raised his hand up high just before the snow swallowed him, hoping to somehow mark the spot.

Will we ever be rescued? Ken wondered. Perhaps I should go for help myself. He shrugged off the thought. Masoud was delirious and in pain. Karim was shaking, his teeth chattering, his skin tinged blue from the cold. The two men were clinging to life, at the mercy of conditions on the mountain. He couldn't leave them, not like this.

Time crawled past. Ken talked to the men, comforting them, sharing information about families, friends, hopes and dreams — anything to keep the men alert, anything to keep their hopes alive. A final avalanche swept down the gully. Luck was with them this time, though. The wave of snow split into two streams above them, bypassing the men and leaving them untouched.

A hiker's nightmare — an avalanche thundering down a slope

Rescuer Ken Rutland on another climbing expedition

More than an hour after the first avalanche, Ken heard the sound of voices, faint at first, then louder as they neared. Rescue teams, at last. The ordeal was over. While spotters uphill kept a watchful eye for further avalanches, emergency workers bundled up the injured men and carried them away.

Ken Rutland is modest about his role in the rescue, and shrugs off the notion that he is somehow special. "Knowing the fears these guys had gave me a lot of courage," Ken explains. "It became a little bit personal — I didn't want to lose them."

To Masoud Shekarchi and Karim Bhatia, though, Ken Rutland is anything but ordinary. Avalanches killed a hiker on Grouse Mountain that day, and without Ken's help these two would have likely died, too. Others have also recognized Ken's bravery. In 1999 he received the Robert P. Connelly Medal for Heroism, and in 2001 he was awarded the Governor General's Star of Courage.

Ken receiving the Star of Courage from Governor General Adrienne Clarkson

Ken feels that the real heroes of Grouse Mountain are the men and women of the search-and-rescue teams who regularly risk their lives to help others in trouble. "There's nothing that I could have done without them that day," he says. Recently, he joined this select group of volunteers. It's his way of giving back something, of recognizing the valuable job that they do.

Because of the events on Grouse Mountain, Ken Rutland has a different outlook on life. "I certainly don't take things for granted anymore," he says. "The most beautiful day could also be the most hazardous day."

Surviving an Avalanche

Avalanches normally occur on steep inclines, usually on the afternoon of a sunny day, and most frequently when new layers of snow fall on top of densely packed older layers. The best precaution is to stay away from avalanche-prone areas. If you must cross one, carry a 2- to 3-metre pole to test snow conditions, and a beacon to broadcast your position should you become covered. Avalanches travel at 80 to 110 kilometres an hour. You cannot outrun an avalanche, but if you keep a clear head you might be able to react quickly enough to survive:

TIPS FOR SURVIVAL

• At the first signs of an avalanche, throw off skis, ski poles, backpacks and other items that might weigh you down.

• Try to stabilize yourself. Grab a sturdy object such as a tree, branch or bush. If you fall, try to move sideways toward the edge of the slide.

• If the snow starts to bury you, thrust yourself upward by using swimming motions. Do your best to stay on top of the snow.

• Reach up with one hand. By leaving one hand above the snow, you mark the area and make your rescue easier.

• If buried by snow, create an air space by moving your head vigorously from side to side.

TORNADO!

The whirling wind blew open the door and seized Dean and Ashley Thomson, ripping them from their seats and sucking them right out of the car.

The Thomson family — Dean, Rachel and their baby, Ashley — pulled through the entrance gates of Green Acres Campground around seven o'clock on Friday evening, around the same time that the wind began its battle. While Rachel ran inside the gatehouse to register, Dean waited at the wheel of their car. Behind him, strapped into her car seat, sat four-month-old Ashley. The Thomsons had come to the popular campground near Red Deer, Alberta, for a family reunion.

Dean glanced out the car window. The sky was a smothering blanket of grey, thick and heavy. Wicked gusts of wind rattled motor homes and trailers, bent branches into pretzel shapes and hurled dust across the road. A storm was on its way.

Suddenly a white streak cut through the clouds, and a barrage of pea-sized hail bounced off the car. There was a dull roar, a sound like a distant train barrelling full-speed down unseen tracks. The wind became more violent and the whole car shook. Dean shifted uneasily. Come on, Rachel. What's keeping you?

Rachel ran out of the gatehouse. She was just a few steps from the car when the wind grew wild. It swept her off her feet and flung her into the bush. Dean watched, frozen behind the wheel, as his wife sailed past.

This was no ordinary wind. It was a tornado.

Dean heard the pop of windows breaking, the sound of glass exploding around him. The whirling wind lifted the car, shook it and twirled it in midair. The car flipped end over end — once, twice, three times. Then all of a sudden the wind let go and the car slammed to the ground. The doors blew open and an incredible force seized Dean, ripping him out of his seat and sucking him out of the car.

Rachel flew through the air. It was thick with shredded metal and shards of broken glass that struck her face and arms, slicing her skin. She bounced off trees. Then, as if tired of playing with her, the wind pitched her to the ground. She grabbed at the grass, clutching it with all her might. Nearby, a motor home exploded into splinters. The once peaceful campground looked like a war zone under full attack.

Dean rode the wind. It tossed him back and forth like a pitcher tossing a ball from hand to hand. He was three storeys above the ground, and from that height he could see across the campground. I must be dead, he thought.

The wind dropped Dean, picked him up again, twirled him, then dropped him again 300 metres away. He lay as flat as possible, gripping roots and branches, anything that would help anchor him to the ground. He prayed for the tornado to pass, but even as he did he could feel the wind tugging at him, spinning him in circles as it tried to yank him free.

The tornado seemed to last forever, but in reality it was only a few minutes. As the wind died, Dean struggled to his feet. He vaguely felt a stab of pain in his left shoulder, but his thoughts were elsewhere. Ashley! Where is she?

Dean made his way through the campground, clambering over broken trees, steering past the twisted metal frames of trailers. He was seized by panic and had to fight to keep his focus. He worked his way back to the crumpled car and peered inside. It was empty. Ashley was nowhere to be seen. She, too, had been sucked out of the car, plucked right out of her baby seat by the tornado.

Dean tore through the wreckage, lifting sheets of siding, pulling aside branches. "Ashley!" he called. "Ashley!" But even as he called, Dean knew that the tornado could have taken Ashley anywhere. Was she nearby, broken and hurt? Or had the tornado swept her away, only to toss her aside in some far-flung field or lake? Was she still alive?

Then he heard a faint cry that sounded like a baby. Desperately he followed the sound. One hundred metres from the car he found Ashley. She was lying under a mound of debris, whimpering softly. Her T-shirt had been ripped off, leaving her wearing only a diaper.

Dean scooped up his daughter and held her close. He found a fluffy coat in a nearby cabin, wrapped it around Ashley and ran to the road to beg a ride from a passing car. Halfway to the Red Deer Hospital, he suddenly thought of Rachel. What had happened to his wife?

As soon as the wind died down, Rachel began her search for her family. She roamed the campground in her bare feet, picking through the mangled remains of campers and trees. Blood dripped from her many cuts and gashes. She felt bruised and sore all over. She tried to find the car, terrified by what she might discover, more afraid of what she might not. Finally she spotted it. The car was crumpled and mashed, partly hidden by branches and splintered wood. It was empty.

"Find my baby!" she screamed. "Find my baby!" Ignoring her own pain, she tore aside branches, ripped away twisted metal, lifted timbers, ran this way and that, finding a strength she didn't know she possessed. Ashley! Dean! They had to be here somewhere. Over and over she screamed, "Help me. Find my baby!"

Rescue workers found her wandering the campground, like a woman possessed. It

Wreckage lies scattered on the ground

took several of them to coax her into an ambulance. It sped to the hospital in Innisfail, a small town not far away. I'm alone now, Rachel thought. I'm the only one left.

———

It was around midnight, a full five hours after the tornado, before Rachel was told that Ashley and Dean were alive. The next day she was moved to the Red Deer Regional Hospital to be with her family. As she held Ashley close to her, she couldn't help but marvel at their good fortune. Her own body was a patchwork of cuts, scrapes and stitches. Dean, meanwhile, was being treated for a broken left shoulder and badly bruised back. Ashley needed two stitches to mend a cut to her foot. But they were alive and together. And that was a miracle.

Not everyone at the Green Acres Campground was as fortunate. The 300-kilometre-an-hour tornado that ripped through it on July 16, 2000, killed eleven people and injured more than 130 others.

Surviving a Tornado

Tornados often follow passing thunderstorms. Before they strike, the wind may die down, and for a short time the air may seem very still. If you are outdoors:

TIPS FOR SURVIVAL

• Seek shelter inside a sturdy building, preferably one with a basement where you can hide.

• If you cannot get indoors, crouch near a building or lie in a ditch or shallow depression.

• Protect your head and neck with your arms.

• Stay out of cars or trucks — tornados can lift and toss them with ease.

KILLER IN THE SHADOWS

Before Jon Nostdal saw the cougar, before he smelled its steamy breath or felt its teeth pierce his scalp, he heard the cat coming.

Hunger drove the cougar to the edge of the road. Hidden among tall grasses and thick bushes, the big cat waited and watched. Its patience was soon rewarded. An unsuspecting animal appeared on the road. The cougar watched it glide past, head low, legs churning. At just the right moment the cat sprang out of the shadows and bounded after it. In seconds, it was behind its prey, ready to pounce, ready to kill.

Jon Nostdal, a fifty-two-year-old tugboat captain, was on his way home. The day had been just about perfect: first a relaxing yoga class, then a satisfying meal at a local restaurant in Port Alice, a village on Vancouver Island. But now Jon needed to return to his ship a few kilometres away. He hopped on his bicycle and headed down the winding road that led to the harbour where his boat was docked. He was unaware of the killer lurking in the shadows.

Before Jon saw the cougar, before he smelled its steamy breath or felt its teeth pierce his scalp, he heard the cat coming. At first he thought it was the sound of his jacket scraping against his backpack, or perhaps the clang of the bicycle chain as he pedalled down the road. But no, the sound was too rhythmical, too steady, to be either one. Like fingers drumming on a tabletop, he heard the click of the cat's claws on the pavement.

Then, just as Jon sensed danger, the cat pounced. Though Jon is a big man, the cougar managed to knock him off his bicycle and throw him to the ground. Before he could react, the cougar had its jaws locked over his skull. Jon fought back. He rolled to one side and pried the animal loose. He struggled to his feet and pounded the cougar with his fists. He shrugged off his backpack and gloves, then tossed them aside, hoping to

distract the animal. But the cougar had only one target in mind. It charged at Jon, throwing its full force at his body.

Jon wrestled with the cougar, but it was a losing battle. The cat raked its claws against his face, and sunk its teeth into his arms and neck. At one point he smashed the cat's head on the pavement, then planted his foot on its neck to pin it to the ground. The cougar snarled and squirmed loose.

After more than five minutes of fighting — five minutes that felt like an eternity — Jon began to weaken. Every time he threw off the cougar, the animal rebounded and attacked again. Blood poured from wounds along Jon's face. He was tiring, and doubts crept into his mind. This is not going well, he told himself. I'm going to die if I don't get help.

The cougar lunged again, this time grabbing Jon from behind. Its right paw clawed Jon's cheek while its left grabbed his shoulder. He struggled to keep his balance, to break away from the cougar's firm grip. The cat screamed in his ear, but above the snarling Jon heard other sounds. Tires on pavement. A door being opened. Shouts.

Elliot Cole, a thirty-nine-year-old mill worker, stopped his truck when he saw the struggle by the side of the road. In a few quick strides he was beside the battling pair. At first he yelled at the cougar, hoping to distract it. When that didn't work, he used his fists to pound the animal. Faster, harder, he rained one blow after another upon the cat. But it kept a steady grip on its prey. Elliot grabbed a bag full of books from the car and used it to clobber the cougar. Finally he picked up Jon's bike and threw it on top of the animal, pinning it to the ground. While the cougar fought to free itself, the two men scrambled to the truck.

Elliot drove Jon to the village hospital, where Jon spent a few days recovering. The attack left him battered, but grateful to the stranger who had come to his rescue. The experience has given him new respect for life, too. "I realize now that it's not at all a given that we are here day to day. Things can end automatically and sometimes brutally."

Surviving a Cougar Encounter

Cougars target small or weak prey. In a confrontation with a cougar, you must convince the animal that you are a threat, not prey:

TIPS FOR SURVIVAL

• Stay calm. Face the cougar and maintain eye contact. Speak loudly and firmly. Do NOT run.

• Try to back away slowly. Do not turn your back on the cougar.

• Make yourself look as big as possible. Stand tall. Get on a rock or stump if possible. Spread your arms. Pick up sticks or branches and wave them about. Do NOT stoop, squat or bend, and do not try to hide.

• If a cougar attacks, fight back with all your might. Use anything to defend yourself, including rocks, sticks, fists, backpacks, fishing poles or cameras.

I'M GOING TO DIE

The crocodile's jaws snapped shut on Val Plumwood. In an instant she was being pulled underwater. I'm going to die, she told herself.

Someone, something, was watching Val Plumwood. The forty-three-year-old woman was convinced of it. Even though she couldn't see anything in the trees and bushes of the swamp, she felt unseen eyes staring at her, following her every move. She shivered. This is spooky, she told herself as she turned the canoe around. I'm going back.

Then suddenly, there it was, around the bend. Two un-blinking yellow eyes peering out of the water, a long gnarly body behind. Her stalker was a crocodile.

Val fought the fear that crawled along her spine. She steered the canoe to the left, hoping to avoid the animal. The crocodile shifted left, too. She paddled to the right. The crocodile followed, blocking her way. There was a loud bang on the side of the canoe. Then another. Impossible, Val thought. Crocodiles don't attack boats. But there was no denying that this one was doing just that, or that she was its chosen prey.

———

Val Plumwood had come to Australia's Kakadu National Park to study its water birds. On a February morning in 1985, she borrowed a 5-metre canoe from a friend, left her trailer at the park ranger station, and headed into the swampy backwaters of the East Alligator River. Despite the light rain, she was looking forward to her day in the wilderness. The area was home to some unusual birds and she loved the solitude and quiet that a canoe trip offered. To avoid treacherous currents, she stayed out of the river's main tributary. Instead she paddled along its shallower, calmer backwaters. She felt safe . . . until her encounter with the crocodile.

Instinct told Val that her chances would be better on land. She paddled hard, aiming the canoe for the muddy bank and

a nearby tree. As the canoe drew close to shore, she jumped, grabbed the lowest tree branch, and pulled herself up.

"Before my foot even tripped the first branch, I had a blurred, incredulous vision of great toothed jaws bursting from the water," Val would write later in "Being Prey," a short story about her encounter. "Then I was seized . . . in a red-hot pincer grip and whirled into the suffocating wet darkness."

Val was pulled under the murky waters, her lower body locked between the clenched jaws of the crocodile. The animal twisted and turned, dragging her to the bottom, then up again. Images flashed through Val's mind, glimmers of facts she had read or heard. Crocodiles drown their prey, rolling them over and over to disorient and daze them. Then, while their prey is weak and defenceless, crocodiles hold them underwater to snuff out their last bit of life.

I'm going to die, Val told herself.

The thrashing continued. No matter how hard she struggled, Val could not break free. She was under water, locked in the crocodile's jaws, her lungs searing with pain and ready to burst.

Without warning, the rolling stopped. The crocodile still

held her tight, but Val discovered that her head was close to the surface. She could stretch just high enough to catch a breath of air. Through the surface of the murky water, she spotted the overhanging branch of a tree. She grabbed the branch and, almost at the same moment, the crocodile let go. Perhaps it was surprised that she was still alive. She wasted no time wondering. She dragged herself along the branch and, like before, pulled herself up the tree.

The crocodile leaped after her. Once more she felt its jaws closing on her. She was ripped from the tree, dragged back into the water, and rolled again and again. She reached for the crocodile, found its gnarly skin, felt for its eyes. If she could jab her fingers into the crocodile's sockets, maybe she could surprise it and make it release her. But her fingers fumbled and failed to find the target.

Then, by chance, Val's hands touched something smooth. It was the tree branch. Once again, she grabbed it. Once again, the crocodile let go and she pulled herself out of the water.

This time she didn't climb the tree. Instead she dragged herself up the slippery bank and collapsed into an exhausted heap. Expecting the worst, she glanced back. There was no sign of the crocodile.

She felt wild excitement. She had escaped. She was alive. But her excitement lasted only seconds. She was badly injured. Her left leg was shredded and a large chunk of flesh was hanging loosely by her side. Somehow she had to find help. She had to get back to the ranger station. And to do that she had to cross the swamp.

She tied her T-shirt around her bleeding leg and staggered through knee-deep water. Daylight was beginning to fade, and she knew that her chances of surviving a night in the swamp would be slim. She half walked, half crawled through the mud, her left leg burning and aching. Her body trembled with shock, and waves of nausea swept over her. She shivered in spite of the Australian heat. Her imagination ran wild. She thought she could hear the crocodile slithering through the swamp, moving closer and closer.

Finally, as the sun was setting, Val reached the edge of the swamp. She could see the ranger station on the other side of a wide stretch of water. The base looked abandoned. She had come so far, struggled so hard, yet now she could go no farther. She stretched out under a tree. All she could do now was wait and hope that someone might find her.

Her pain was intense, and Val began to wish that she would pass out. But she worried about the crocodile, too. Was it lurking nearby, waiting for a chance to finish her off? She struggled to stay alert. Her survival depended on it. If anyone came looking for her, she had to be able to call to them.

In her delirious state, Val thought she saw lights flash across the water. Is that the sound of a motor? she wondered. She raised herself up and yelled with all her might, "Help! Help!"

There was a long pause, then she heard the sweetest sound of all. "Stay there. We're coming to get you!" A ranger at the base had noticed that she was missing, and was about to set out on a search on his motorcycle. Val's cry came at just the right time. Within a half-hour, someone was by Val's side, helping her into a boat, hurrying her to a hospital.

━━━

Val has strong memories of her encounter with the crocodile. Her leg is crisscrossed with thick scars, reminders of many painful skin grafts and hours of physiotherapy. But more than anything it is her dreams that remind her. In her most vivid nightmares, the crocodile returns to hunt her again.

Surviving Crocodilians

Crocodiles and alligators can be found in many tropical areas around the world, but South Florida is the only place where both can be found together. The Florida Game and Fresh Water Fish Commission and the Florida Park Service recommend these precautions when dealing with crocodilians, the family group to which both alligators and crocodiles belong:

TIPS FOR SURVIVAL

• Keep your distance. Stay at least 25 metres away. These reptiles can sprint at lightning speeds for short distances.

• Never swim, or walk dogs or small children in alligator- or crocodile-infested areas, especially at twilight or at night. These are prime times for attack.

• Never feed an alligator or crocodile. History has shown that in the majority of attacks, the crocodilian in question had been fed by humans prior to the incident.

• If you find a crocodilian nest on shore, quickly retreat. Mothers aggressively defend their nests.

• If you are the victim of an attack, and are unable to escape by running away, fight back by pounding the creature's eyes and snout with any weapon you have: sticks, stones, a knife, a soda can, even your fist.

• Once you are freed, seek medical help immediately. The crocodilian mouth is filled with bacteria, and serious infection is a real possibility.

ANGEL BY HIS SIDE

*Mark Durrance felt something
curved and fleshy underfoot. Almost
in the same instant, crushing
pressure seized him and searing
pain shot up his leg.*

Twelve-year-old Mark Durrance and his dog Bobo were hunting. It was small game mostly — rabbit, the occasional gopher, a bird or two — whatever they could find scrambling through the dry grass behind their isolated home in southwestern Florida.

On this lazy Sunday afternoon in February, the boy carried a BB gun. With Bobo's help he scoured the brush, hoping to flush an animal into the open. When he spotted a bird on the other side of a drainage ditch, Mark jumped across for a closer look. As he landed he felt something curved and fleshy underfoot. Almost in the same instant, crushing pressure seized him and searing pain shot up his leg.

Mark dropped the gun and wheeled around for a look. He caught a glimpse of a large brown head, its massive jaws spread wide over his right foot, its fangs buried deep into his shoe. From the diamond pattern crisscrossing its body, Mark knew it was an Eastern diamondback rattlesnake, one of the world's deadliest.

Bobo flew into a frenzy of barking and nipping. He charged the snake, retreated, then charged again. With each attack, the snake tightened its grip on Mark. There seemed to be no way to shake it loose. Finally Bobo pounced and ripped into the snake's head, drawing blood. The snake let go and slithered away.

Mark tried calling out for help, but his voice sounded rusty and he managed only a faint croak. A rush of heat surged through him. He felt dizzy, wobbly, unsure of where his own feet were. He teetered, and the ground rushed toward him. He slammed into the dirt, a crumpled heap of arms and legs.

The snake's aim had been deadly accurate. Its fangs had punctured a main artery, so the venom had been injected directly into Mark's bloodstream. It raced through his body, seeping into cells, spreading into tissues, thinning his blood and attacking organs. Already his heart was faltering, and his lungs were desperately trying to contain oxygen.

Mark looked down the path toward the house, more than 140 metres away. The building looked hazy, like an out-of-focus snapshot. He could barely make out Bobo dancing in front of him, yelping urgently to get his attention. I'll never make it, not like this, he thought.

What happened next is something Mark cannot forget. He says he saw a white-robed figure step from the shadows. You'll make it . . . trust me . . . he heard a deep voice say. Suddenly, he felt buoyant, his feet no longer a plodding weight. Was he floating or being carried down the path, past the shrubbery bordering the house, up the thirteen steps leading to the door?

From the kitchen, Debbie Durrance heard the front door open and her older son, Buddy, shout, "Mark, what's wrong?" Debbie froze when she heard Mark answer, "I've been rattlesnake bit." She dropped everything and raced to the living room, arriving just as Mark swayed and collapsed to the floor.

Debbie tore off Mark's shoe. His foot was purple and swollen. A strong, musky odour filled the room, an odour Debbie recognized immediately as the smell of snake venom mingling with flesh. "Go get your father. Hurry!" she shouted to Buddy.

Bobby Durrance, Mark's father, was outdoors pruning bushes. He dropped everything and followed Buddy to the house. Mark was on the floor with his mother at his side. He was twitching uncontrollably, his entire body a trembling knot of convulsions.

The Durrances had no telephone, and no nearby neighbours to call for help. The closest clinic was 27 kilometres away. Quickly they tied a tourniquet around Mark's leg to stem the flow of poison. Then Bobby gathered Mark in his arms and ran to the pickup truck.

Bobby drove down the highway at breakneck speed, weaving through traffic, passing cars that were too slow, honking at those that got in his way. Beside him, Debbie cradled Mark. He was limp. His breathing was shallow, almost unnoticeable.

Two kilometres from the clinic, the engine sputtered. Steam poured from under the hood, as the truck overheated. When Bobby braked for another vehicle, the engine died altogether and the truck rolled to a stop. Bobby jumped out, stood in the middle of the road and waved his arms to attract attention. In desperation he gathered Mark in his arms, held him high and wandered into traffic.

An old car braked and screeched to a halt. The driver was an immigrant farm worker with little English, but he understood Debbie's frantic motions. He drove them to the clinic at top speed. By that time Mark had lapsed into a coma.

Doctors injected fluids and started artificial respiration in an attempt to stabilize Mark's condition. Then he was transferred by ambulance to a hospital 16 kilometres away. There, doctors and nurses hovered over his seemingly lifeless body. To relieve the pressure on his bloated leg, they slashed it from top to bottom. They hooked him up to a respirator to force air into his lungs, and they gave him massive transfusions. Mark was injected with an antivenin serum to counteract the snake venom.

Debbie and Bobby Durrance waited at Mark's side, praying and talking to him. Mark no longer looked like the fair-haired boy who had gone off hunting earlier that day. His entire body was swollen. His hands were three times their normal size and his face was so puffy that his eyes seemed like narrow slits in his bulging flesh. Blood seeped from every opening — eyes, ears, mouth, even the pores of his skin.

Sunday edged into Monday, then Monday into Tuesday. Mark's condition stabilized, but he remained unconscious. Then, on Wednesday, four days after his encounter with the snake, Mark emerged from the coma. He was groggy, his voice raspy and unsteady, but he was alert enough to tell his story.

He told of stepping on the snake, of Bobo's heroic actions, of the weakness and helplessness that he felt. Then he told his startled family about the white-robed stranger who had appeared out of nowhere, the stranger who had saved his life.

Mark eventually made a full recovery. That in itself was a miracle, for few people survive a direct attack from an Eastern diamondback rattlesnake. But Mark claimed another miracle occurred that fateful Sunday. He is convinced that an angel stepped out of the shadows to give him a hand when he needed it most.

Treating Snake Bite

If you should be bitten by a venomous snake, keep these points in mind. They may save your life.

TIPS FOR SURVIVAL

• Keep the wounded area still, and if possible, lower than your heart. This will help slow the flow of poison through your body.

• Seek medical help as soon as possible.

• If help is not immediately available, tie a bandage, sock or other piece of clothing 5 to 10 centimetres above the bite to slow the spread of venom. Do NOT tie so tightly, however, that the blood flow is completely restricted.

• Do not suck out the venom. You do not want more venom to enter your system.

TERROR IN THE DEEP

Pinned to his surfboard by the great white shark, his body numb from shock, blood trailing from the massive wound, Andy Carter screamed and prepared to die.

Andy Carter sometimes wakes up in the dead of night, his heart pounding, his body drenched in sweat. In dreams that seem as real as life itself, he swims, trying to keep ahead of the monster and its gaping jaws. But the monster is gaining on him. Andy can see its vacant black eyes as it lunges at him. He screams as rows of razor-sharp teeth sink into his skin, and the great white shark rips him in two.

Waking up is the only way to survive. Andy sits bolt upright, waiting for the terror to subside. It's only a dream, he tells himself. Then his hand drifts down to his left thigh and his fingers touch the scars that crisscross his leg. *This* time it's only a dream.

The dreams started after an especially hot Saturday in June of 1994. The sky was blue, the sun a blazing furnace. Like dozens of others that day, Andy — a surfer — went to the beach near his home in South Africa. He paddled his surfboard about 200 metres offshore, then lay face down, waiting to catch the perfect wave.

All at once, he felt a massive tug and crushing pressure on his left leg. Fear rose in his throat. He knew without looking that it was a shark, but he reacted calmly in spite of the terror that seized him. He twisted his neck and glanced back. He saw a huge black head and immense jaws more than a metre wide. The jaws were clamped around the surfboard, the shark's teeth embedded deep in his thigh. Blood poured from the wound, staining the water red.

Pinned to his surfboard, far from shore, his body numb from shock, Andy was powerless to fight back. He screamed and prepared to die.

Other surfers heard Andy's screams. What they saw horrified them. The shark was so large, its jaws so wide, that it seemed to be tearing Andy in half. Convinced there was no way to help him, most turned and paddled to shore, frantic to save themselves.

Andy gripped the board tightly. Then, the first of several unexpected things happened. The shark suddenly opened its mouth, let go of him, then lunged again to take a bigger bite of its prey. In that split second the surfboard somehow twisted, turned and wedged itself in the shark's jaws. Andy reacted swiftly. He slid off the board and swam for his life.

Far from shore, Andy was in the shark's domain. His only chance to survive was to reach shallower waters. With blood trailing behind him and his left leg dragging uselessly, he used his arms to pull himself through the water. Now and then he checked over his shoulder. He couldn't see the shark, but he knew it wasn't far away. It had tasted Andy's blood and wouldn't give up easily.

Although in top physical shape from years of surfing, Andy was weakening quickly. He felt like passing out. I'll never make it, he thought. Not like this. He glanced back. No shark, but he could see the battered surfboard bobbing in the water. He turned around and paddled toward it. He grabbed hold, dragged himself out of the water and lay there, too exhausted to move.

The shoreline seemed so far away. Impossibly far, Andy thought. But then, a second unexpected thing happened. A wave caught the surfboard and carried it to shore.

Andy crawled to a rock next to the beach, blood pouring from his leg. He pressed on the wound, hoping to stop the flow. To his surprise, his hand disappeared into the open flesh. The shark had bitten almost through his thigh. His injuries were more serious than he had first realized and he knew he was in danger of bleeding to death. Any movement would only increase the bleeding. All he could do was lie still and hope for help — no one seemed to have noticed that he had washed ashore.

Andy's vision began to blur as his body drifted into shock. He scanned the beach and noticed two faint images on the sand — two girls out to get a tan. He called to them, hoping they could hear him.

He was barely alert by the time the two girls reached his side. He told them to pack clothes and towels into his wound and then to bind his leg. By now, he was drifting into unconsciousness. His rescuers looked hazy, and their voices sounded distant and hollow. The events from his life flowed past him in an endless parade. In this foggy state, he was barely aware that paramedics had arrived and he was being whisked away.

Andy woke up in hospital after five hours of surgery. It had taken 400 stitches to sew his body back together. It was only then that he found out about Bruce Corby, and the most tragic and freakish event of the whole day.

Bruce Corby was one of the few surfers who had remained in the water after Andy's attack. Thwarted by Andy's escape, the shark had turned and hunted for new prey. It had caught Bruce and bitten off his right leg at the knee. Bruce had fought his way back to the beach, but his injuries were too severe,

Andy Carter with scars on his thigh and his ruined surfboard

the loss of blood too great. He stopped breathing.

Andy slowly recovered from the attack, but memories of the shark's attack have never quite left him. The great white shark returns to haunt him in dreadful dreams, and when he goes swimming — as he still does — the terror of that day sometimes returns. He senses the shark's presence and knows that the monster is never far away.

Avoiding a Shark Attack

There are several steps you can take to lessen the chances of a shark attack:

TIPS FOR SURVIVAL

• Stay in groups. Sharks are more likely to attack a solitary person.

• Avoid being in the water during darkness or twilight hours when sharks are more active.

• Wear dull, muted colours. Sharks see sharp contrasts and bright colours particularly well.

• Avoid wearing shiny jewellery. To a shark, the light reflecting from jewellery may resemble the glimmer of fish scales.

• Do not wander far from shore. The farther away you are, the more isolated and vulnerable you become.

• If a shark attacks, hit back with your fist, your camera — anything you happen to have on hand. Aim for its eyes or gills and make quick, powerful jabs at these targets.

NO TIME TO ESCAPE

Before Bram knew it, the grizzly was on top of him, its immense mouth clamped around his head, gnawing it like a walnut about to be crushed.

There was no real reason for the attack, it seemed. It came from nowhere — sudden, swift and deadly. There was no time to climb a tree to escape the razor-sharp claws, or grab the rifle and take aim at the charging animal. Barely enough time to take four quick but useless steps. Then, *wham!* The grizzly was on top of Bram Schaffer, its immense mouth clamped around his head, gnawing it like a walnut about to be crushed.

Bram, a wiry eighteen-year-old, fell to the ground and began the fight of his life. While the 180-kilogram bear straddled his legs, pinning him down, Bram flailed his arms, punching the grizzly with all the force he could muster. Enraged, the bear tore into his left arm.

Through the pain and panic, a thought flashed through Bram's mind. The gun! He spotted the rifle, but it was underneath the bear. He stretched out his right arm, fumbling in the dirt, hoping to feel the coolness of the rifle barrel. But again there was no time. The grizzly released his arm, trading it for Bram's left thigh. The beer's teeth sank deep into the flesh, and lifted its victim. "She had my left thigh in her mouth and was shaking me around like a dog would a dish towel," Bram later told a friend. He thought he heard the snap of breaking bones.

Then, for no apparent reason, the bear suddenly released its hold, dropping Bram to the ground. It turned and sauntered back to the young cub it had left behind. Bram reached for the rifle, and not a moment too soon. Hearing its prey move, the bear turned and charged again. This time Bram was ready. He took aim, fired one shot, and brought the animal down. The bear was dead, killed by a single well-placed bullet.

Bram's nightmare was just beginning. His down-filled jacket was shredded, and its feathers floated to the ground like snowflakes. A hunk of flesh the size of a dinner roast was missing from his right side. His hand and wrist were mangled, and blood gushed from wounds on his scalp. Worst of all was his left thigh. Raw muscle had been peeled and pulled from the bone, and it now it hung and flapped from his leg like meat hanging in a butcher shop.

"My leg didn't really hurt," Bram said later. "It scared me when I looked at it, but I got a grip." Bram tucked the muscle back into his tattered jeans, then took off his hunting vest and tied it around his leg to hold the flesh in place.

An eerie silence settled over the woods. Bram pushed back the pain and tried to collect his thoughts. It was the 1995 elk-hunting season around Horseshoe Mountain, a wilderness area just north of Yellowstone National Park. An hour earlier Bram had left his hunting party to head out on his own. Now it was almost five in the afternoon, and, since it was past mid-

September, nightfall was fast approaching. The sky was grey and rain fell steadily. Temperatures hovered around freezing, threatening to turn the rain into snow at any moment.

Bram's situation was desperate. He was alone, far from help, and mortally wounded. Night, with all its hidden horrors, was just around the corner. No one from his hunting party — not even his father — knew of his exact whereabouts.

▬▬

Farther up the mountain, Dennis Schaffer, Bram's father, and others in the group gathered around a campfire. This was the rendezvous point they had set up days earlier. At a higher altitude the air was colder, and already snow drifted from the overcast sky, covering the mushy ground with a thick layer of cleansing white. Although Bram was the youngest in the party, he was an experienced hunter, wise in the ways of the woods, not one to lose his way. So when his son didn't show up by nightfall, Dennis knew something was seriously wrong.

The hunting party went looking for Bram, scouring the forest, firing signal shots every few dozen paces. They listened, hoping to hear him fire back. But the woods were dark and quiet.

▬▬

Bram knew that to stay in one spot meant certain death. He would bleed to death or die from shock. He had to move, had to somehow find the others and get the help he so urgently needed. They would be looking for him, he was sure, and if he kept moving perhaps their paths would cross. With his leg damaged and bundled, however, he could only hobble in an awkward, stiff-legged way. That ruled out going back uphill the way he had come. He could go downhill, though.

With his rifle in hand, he staggered down the rough trail. In the growing darkness he stumbled over stones, slithered under deadfall and crawled past rock outcroppings that blocked his way. Occasionally he heard gunshots in the distance. Bram fired his own rifle in reply, but the sound of his shots was muffled by the trees and lost to the rising wind.

Conditions on the mountain worsened. The wind whipped the falling snow into drifts, and temperatures plunged. Dennis

Schaffer and the others in his party searched for hours before calling it quits and heading back to camp. It was simply too dangerous to continue. But Dennis found it impossible to rest. The night was an endless nightmare. Bram was out there somewhere, wounded, lost, perhaps already dead.

Bram was desperate by this point. He had walked for hours, covering 3 or 4 kilometres, staggering and stumbling forward. Chills ran through his body and the cold sapped his strength. Around 8:30 p.m., he heard a rifle shot. It echoed through the woods, loud and clear. It came from somewhere nearby. Quickly Bram fired a return shot.

"Over here," a voice called.

"Help! Help!" Bram screamed. "I've been attacked by a grizzly!" He was weak, and so soaked in sweat that steam rose like foggy clouds from his body.

Two men emerged from the woods. Bruce and Bryce Piasecki, a father-and-son team out hunting, were on their way back to rendezvous with the others in their group. Bruce took off his raincoat, put it on Bram, and tied the hood down to stop the bleeding from his head. Then he rebandaged Bram's leg, tucking in the leg muscle and securing it tightly.

Hoisting Bram onto his strong back, Bruce stumbled through the woods with Bryce leading the way. In the darkness the trail was difficult to see, and several times Bruce slipped, jarring Bram and causing him to scream in pain. Bruce talked to Bram, trying to keep him alert and alive.

At one point Bruce, exhausted, stopped to rest. "I felt like I couldn't go on any more and I prayed to God for help," he said later. "I picked him up and almost started running with him. I got a burst of energy like you wouldn't believe. He didn't feel heavy any more."

After Bruce had carried Bram for more than a kilometre, the three men finally encountered two other hunters, one of them a doctor. Together they half-carried, half-walked Bram to their camp. While one of them set off on horseback to contact the ranger, the doctor treated Bram, administering painkillers and washing out the wounds with disinfectant and detergent. He applied sterile bandages and secured Bram's arm to his side, hoping to stem the flow of blood.

The night passed slowly. With the wild and unpredictable weather, travel was impossible, and help was a long way off. Bram huddled under blankets, tossing and turning restlessly while the others kept an eye on his condition. Bram's leg felt hot and puffy, a sign that deadly infection was beginning to set in.

A helicopter arrived early the next morning to whisk Bram off to a hospital in Billings, Montana. Dennis was located and given the news. He left the camp immediately and drove to the hospital, arriving around five o'clock that afternoon, a full twenty-four hours after his son was attacked.

Bram spent four days in intensive care and another month in the hospital undergoing three operations to repair the damage to his leg. Doctors cut away the dead and infected tissue, and skin from Bram's right leg was grafted over the wounds in his left. All told, Bram lost about 35 percent of his thigh. Even though he will likely walk with a limp for the rest of his life, he knows he is lucky.

He survived a grizzly attack, plain and simple.

Surviving a Bear Attack

One of the best ways to survive an attack, of course, is to avoid bear encounters in the first place. If you're in an area where you might spot a bear, make plenty of noise, travel in groups, keep on the lookout, store food only in approved containers, and stay away from carrion. Before travelling where bears might be around, check with the closest ranger station for full information about how to stay safe.

Bear attacks are rare. Bears usually attack only if they're surprised or forced to defend themselves, their young, or their food. The best defence if you encounter a bear is to stay calm, back away slowly, and try to leave the area. According to Parks Canada, how you should react if a bear attacks depends upon the *reason* for the attack:

• If you surprise a bear and it attacks you in self-defence, play dead. Lie on your stomach with legs apart. Protect your face, the back of your head and your neck with your arms. Remain still. Usually these attacks last only a few minutes. If the attack continues for more than a few minutes, consider fighting back. Sometimes this discourages the bear, causing it to leave.

• If a bear stalks you and then attacks, or if it attacks at night, first try to escape to a building, into a car, or up a tree. If you cannot escape, use bear spray, shout or try to intimidate the bear with a branch or rock. Do not act passive; make yourself look larger and more dominant. Do whatever you can to let the bear know you are not easy prey.

TIPS FOR SURVIVAL

CLINGING TO LIFE

Carolina Pedro had climbed the tree to escape the flood, but the pregnant woman was going into labour. The baby was on its way.

Carolina slept fitfully. The twenty-six-year-old mother had much on her mind — the rain, the rising river, the baby that was due any day.

It was the monsoon season of 2000 in Mozambique, Africa, and throughout the month of February the rain had been constant. The ground around Carolina's village was saturated with water, and the nearby Limpopo River strained against its muddy banks. On top of it all, Carolina was nine months pregnant. Any day she would deliver her third child in the wet and soggy conditions.

In the middle of the night a shudder shook Carolina's small hut, jolting her awake. Immediately she sensed something was wrong. Above the patter of rain on the thatched roof, above the soft breathing of her husband, Benet, and their two children, Carolina heard other, more troubling sounds — the rush of water, the creaking and groaning of timbers beneath the hut.

Carolina knew in an instant that the river had overflowed its banks. Floodwaters were sweeping over the ground, tearing away the soil, and ripping the wooden foundations from under the hut. Before she had time to act, the hut swayed and toppled. The entire back wall collapsed, plunging a corner of the hut into the river. In seconds Carolina and her family were knee-deep in the raging water.

They ran for their lives, leaving everything behind in their flight. The water was rising quickly, and the current was swift and strong. They fought its pull and plowed through the water, not sure where to go. They were not alone. Cries of terror filled the night and the swirling water was alive with others who were fleeing to safety. The Pedros reached a large tree,

Flood survivors being evacuated from a rooftop

one of many along the banks of the river. Clawing for a hold, they fought their way up its thick trunk and into its high branches. Carolina was relieved to find her parents and Benet's among the dozen people who had made it to safety in the tree.

Suddenly, she was startled by a cry. She heard a scream, and from the corner of her eye saw her mother lose her hold on the tree and fall into the water. In no time, the woman was swept away. There was nothing anyone could do to save her. Each person in the tree must have shared the same thought. Who would be next to fall into the river?

Throughout the long night Carolina and the others clung to the tree as the rain pelted them and the river edged ever higher. Dawn revealed a horrible sight. As far as they could see, water surrounded them. Their village was gone. Books, furniture and clothing littered the water. Only bits and pieces of their former lives remained. Here and there, bloated bodies swirled past in a grotesque watery dance of death.

As the day dragged by Carolina and her family grew increasingly tired, hungry and thirsty. The branches were wet and slippery. The children cried and Carolina consoled them, telling them that here in the tree they were safe, and that soon they would be rescued. Secretly, though, she worried. How long could they hang on? Would anyone come to rescue them? Without food, water and sleep, they couldn't last forever. Carolina wedged herself in a crotch in the tree. She was exhausted and her body, heavy with the child inside her, begged for rest.

Two long days and nights passed. The situation in the tree grew more desperate. There was no sign of rescue. Hunger gnawed at the stomachs of the villagers, and their mouths felt pasty dry. They were afraid of falling out of the tree, but the need to quench their thirst was greater. Holding on to each other, they climbed down the tree to drink the polluted water.

By the fourth day Carolina's entire body ached. Her belly felt heavier than usual, and pains shot along her back. From her previous pregnancies, Carolina understood what was happening. She was going into labour. The tree was no place to deliver a child, but the river was as high and swift as ever. The baby was on its way and there was nothing Carolina could do about it. She prayed for her unborn child. She prayed for rescue.

Once or twice in the previous days, the villagers in the tree had heard helicopters swooping over the river. Now they thought they heard another. It sounded close, and through the thick foliage they could make out the tiny form of a chopper in the distance. Would the pilot see them? Carolina's brother-in-law climbed higher up the tree and waved a white shirt, hoping to attract the pilot's attention.

It worked. The helicopter veered their way and hovered overhead. Using a winch, the rescuers lowered a medic into the tree. But the whirling blades of the helicopter churned the air, whipping the tree, shaking it from top to bottom. Carolina remembered her mother falling. She could still hear her

Carolina and little Rositha, two days after their rescue

screams as the river sucked her under. Frozen in fear, Carolina hung on with all her might.

The medic had to assess the situation quickly. Carolina was in full labour and could not be moved. She needed a doctor. For now, all he could do was airlift Carolina's children to safety. As they were hoisted into the helicopter, he motioned to Carolina that he would return with help. In her heart, Carolina knew she could not wait. The baby's head was already making its way through the birth canal. She clenched a branch tightly, and with the help of other villagers she prepared to give birth. By the time the chopper returned with the doctor, Carolina had a new daughter at her side. Carolina named her baby Rositha, after her mother.

———

Carolina and her baby made headlines worldwide. Thousands of people died in the flood that swept Mozambique, but the story of Rositha, the baby born in a tree, offered survivors new hope in their troubled times.

Surviving a Flash Flood

Flash floods occur quickly, usually after the ground becomes saturated and unable to hold more water. If a flash flood WATCH is issued for your area, be alert and ready to evacuate on a moment's notice. If a flash flood WARNING is issued, the danger is immediate — act quickly to save yourself.

TIPS FOR SURVIVAL

• Go to higher ground. Get out of low-lying areas such as dips, valleys and canyons. Climb to safety.

• Walk around flooded areas rather than through them. Do not attempt to cross fast-flowing streams. Just 10 centimetres of swiftly moving water can be enough to sweep you off your feet.

• If driving, turn around and go another way when you come to a flooded area. Never drive through flooded roadways.

• Be alert to changes in road conditions. Flood waters can tear away at the subsoil, leaving even the firmest looking pavement fragile and weak underneath.

• If your car stalls, leave it immediately and climb to higher ground. Rapidly rising water can literally swallow cars, sweeping them and their occupants downstream.

• Keep tuned to a battery-operated radio for the latest information about evacuation routes and safety procedures.

THROUGH THE ICE

*The snowmobile slid out of control,
plunging into the frigid water,
carrying the two friends with it.*

Angela Paulson still bears scars from the fateful night of February 3, 2001. Her feet are gnarled from frostbite, and at times it hurts her to walk. But the pain goes deeper than that, and it's more than just physical. It's tied to dark memories that are difficult to shake.

That Saturday night, Angela and her close friend, Scott Davidson, were at a house party on Rabbit Lake, about fifteen minutes from their homes in Kenora, Ontario. Eighteen-year-old Angela had come with her younger sister. Twenty-three-year-old Scott had arrived by snowmobile. Around midnight, the two left the party and headed home.

Scott was wearing a heavy snowmobile suit. Angela wore jeans, several sweaters, hiking boots and mitts. Just before leaving, Scott gave Angela his own jeans and ski mask, and found a heavy winter coat for her. He warned her that the ride home on the snowmobile would be a chilly one.

To save a few minutes, Scott took a shortcut across the lake, a route he had used before. This time, though, the ice was different. It was slushy and peppered with stretches of open water. Partway across the lake, the snowmobile began to slip and sink. Scott gunned the engine, but the machine slid out of control, plunged into the frigid water and disappeared in a great gulp below the surface.

Angela's waterlogged clothes dragged her down. Frantically she kicked and paddled to stay afloat. The hood of her coat covered her eyes, and not being able to see increased her panic. She screamed hysterically. Then she heard Scott. He was in the water beside her, speaking quietly, offering encouragement. His voice was so calm, so soothing, that Angela drew strength from it.

She clawed at the ice, trying to pull herself out. But the ice was brittle. It snapped into razor-sharp bits and soon her knuckles were raw and bleeding.

"We aren't going to make it," she sobbed.

"Sure we will," she heard Scott answer.

Again and again, she tried . . . and failed. Then, with exhaustion sweeping through her body, Angela grabbed a solid edge of ice. She hauled herself out and rolled away from the hole. "Over here, Scott," she screamed. "The ice is okay over here." She started to move back toward Scott, and toward the hole in the ice.

"Stay back from the edge," Scott yelled back. "Go back, Angie."

But she wouldn't listen. She crept closer to the place where she had pulled herself out of the water. When Scott paddled over to the same spot, she helped him out.

For a few minutes they lay on the ice, too weak to move. Angela closed her eyes. Sleep was so near, so inviting, it was hard to resist. When she twisted her head to look at Scott, she felt a tug and heard a crack like a twig being broken. It was her long hair, so frozen and so brittle that it snapped as she ripped it off the ice. That's when Angela knew they had to move. Move or freeze to death — it was as simple as that.

Holding each other, they shuffled to shore. In the distance they could see the faint shadow of a cabin, so they headed there. Scott had lost both boots and his socks were frozen to his feet like an extra layer of skin. Angela's fingers and toes were beyond numb. The legs of her jeans were so cardboard stiff that she could hear them scraping together with each step. The two friends fell, stumbled to their feet, fell again. Scott, ever the light-hearted one, cracked jokes and offered encouragement, but Angela noticed that his voice sounded weak. He was having trouble speaking.

Hypothermia was setting in. With their body temperatures plunging, Scott and Angela shivered uncontrollably. Their muscles stiffened and each step became an exhausting burden. Hypothermia muddles the mind, causing confusion and creating illusions, so their brains had grown foggy, too. They waded through waist-deep snow like robots moving through thick molasses.

The cabin was locked and deserted. With her elbow, Angela smashed the glass pane of the door and the two crawled out of the blowing wind. They searched the pitch-black cabin, hoping to find blankets, matches, firewood — anything that would help them fend off the incredible cold. Finally they found a blanket and huddled under it. They clawed at their frozen clothes, desperate

Angela Paulson

to shed them, but their socks and pants were cemented to their bodies.

Throughout the night, Scott told jokes and tried to keep Angela's spirits high. They were afraid to sleep, afraid they might never wake up again. But sleep was impossible to ignore.

By morning, Scott was barely conscious. Angela fought the muddiness that gripped her mind, the awful chill that reduced her movements to slow-motion jerks. She crawled through the cabin, hoping that by daylight she might discover something they had overlooked the night before. She found a phone. Her fingers were numb, shaking uncontrollably, barely able to find the holes on the rotary dial. She dialled zero and got the emergency operator.

By this time, Angela's mind was a tangled web of confusion. It was so hard to think, so hard to answer the operator's questions, when all she really wanted to do was curl up beside Scott and let sleep take over.

Where was the cabin? What did it look like? Angela really couldn't recall. The operator told her to check on Scott. Don't let him sleep, she was told. Keep him alert at all costs. Tell him that help is on the way.

"Are you okay?" Angela yelled to him, still on the phone. "Talk to me, Scott." But Scott had already lost consciousness. Angela shook him, screamed at him, tried to snap him awake. Then, when he stopped breathing, she tried CPR.

At some point in the confusion, Angela hung up the phone. When she heard it ring later, she grabbed it, thinking it was the operator returning her call. It wasn't. By some freak chance, it was the owner of the cabin, merely calling to see if the line was open. The owner called the police and gave them directions to the cabin. In less than an hour, two rescuers were at the door. They wrapped Scott and Angela in blankets, and whisked them to the hospital.

For Angela, the next few hours are hazy and difficult to recall. She remembers the doctors and nurses hovering over her, giving her aid, thawing her body, tending to her severely frost-bitten fingers and toes. But the most painful memory from the hospital has nothing to do with skin, muscle or bone. It comes from the moment when her dad visited her, when he sat on the bed beside her, held her hand tenderly in his own, and broke the news. Scott's heart had failed. It was too late to save him. All the medical help in the world couldn't bring him back.

At first, Angela refused to accept the news. "I thought I was in the middle of a bad dream, that I would wake up any minute and it would be over."

But it wasn't. As reality seeped in, Angela collapsed. She fell out of the hospital bed and lay on the floor, rocking and screaming uncontrollably, calling for her friend but knowing that he was far, far away, and would never return.

She did go to Scott's funeral, a decision that she now realizes was a good one. The minister who officiated at the service had visited Angela in the hospital. Together they had talked about Scott. When the minister spoke at the funeral of Scott the jokester, Scott the loyal friend, Scott the brave companion, Angela heard the echo of her own words.

Somehow that has helped her on the long road to recovery.

Dealing with Thin Ice

Ice on lakes, rivers and streams is never completely safe or predictable. Ice that is 20 centimetres thick in one spot might be just a few centimetres thick an arm's length away. The best advice is this: STAY OFF THE ICE. It is never safe. However, if you must venture across the ice, keep these tips in mind:

TIPS FOR SURVIVAL

• Stay away from cracks, seams, ridges and slushy patches where ice may be weak.

• Watch out for darker patches that indicate areas of thin ice.

• As a general rule, 10 to 15 centimetres of solid ice are needed to support a single person; much thicker ice is required for a snowmobile.

• If you break through the ice, work your way back to the point where you fell in. Remember, the ice in that direction was solid enough to hold you.

• To manoeuvre out of the water, place your hands and arms on the unbroken ice and work forward by kicking your feet. Once you are onto unbroken ice, roll away to more solid areas or push yourself forward on your stomach. (Lying flat spreads your weight over a larger surface, lessening the pressure and decreasing the chances of breaking the ice.)

STRANDED IN HELL

The three men were surrounded by poisonous fumes and bubbling lava inside Kilauea, the world's most frequently erupting volcano.

Saturday November 21, 1992, was another rainy day in Hawaii's Volcano National Park, not the best of days for flying over Mount Kilauea, the world's most active volcano. Certainly it wasn't a great day for shooting movie footage of the crater floor. But after waiting a week for the sky to clear, Hollywood filmmaker Michael Benson could wait no longer. "Let's go," Michael told his companions, camera technician Chris Duddy and helicopter pilot Craig Hosking.

Steam rose in hazy plumes from Kilauea, and low clouds clung to its jagged peaks. Craig steered the helicopter into the crater, circling low and wide, hoping for a clear view of the vents and bubbling lava pots below. He hovered, giving Michael and Chris a chance to shoot a few seconds of film.

Suddenly a warning light on the instrument panel flashed. The helicopter sputtered, lost power and began to fall. "We have a problem," Craig announced calmly. "We're going down." The crater floor was pocked with red-hot lava pools and immense boulders. Craig gripped the controls tightly, hoping to steer past them. But as he neared the ground the main rotor clipped a large rock. The helicopter crashed to a jarring stop less than 100 metres from a pool of molten lava.

The men were shaken, but unharmed. The helicopter, however, was damaged beyond repair. Its tail was broken, its batteries smashed and useless. There was no way to fly out, no power for the radio, and no possibility of being seen from the air through the dense clouds. Not that anyone would come looking for them anyway. They weren't due back for another hour.

The air was heavy with sulphurous gases. The men could hardly breathe. There was only one chance for survival —

Sulphurous gases can be as deadly as lava

climb out of the crater. Head past the boiling lava, sidestep hot spots in the thin crust and scramble up the steep slope to the rim some 180 metres overhead.

It was an impossible climb. The sides of the crater angled sharply. The surface was covered in deep ash and shards of rock, making it slippery and treacherous. Partway up, Chris, who was in the lead, found his way blocked by an overhanging rock. "I can't go any farther. Don't come this way," he shouted to the others.

The men weighed the options. They could stay where they

were and hope for a rescue. In the meantime, though, there was a good chance they might fall to their deaths or suffocate from the fumes. Besides, anyone daring enough to attempt a rescue wouldn't know where to look for them.

There was one other choice. It was dangerous, and only one of the three men had the skill to do it. Craig could head back to the helicopter situated down the slippery slope and through the poisonous gases. He could tinker with the radio, get it working again and call for help.

"My going back is our only hope," Craig told the others. Over their objections, he headed back into the crater.

––––

Craig skidded down the slope. The fumes grew thicker and more choking with each step. When he reached the crater floor, he ripped off his shirt and wrapped it around his face like a scarf. His eyes watering, he fumbled his way to the helicopter.

With its batteries smashed the radio was useless, but Craig had a sudden brainstorm.

He found the movie camera and removed its battery. With some clever wiring perhaps he could hook it up to the radio and get it running. He spliced the wires of the camera battery to the radio. The task was normally an easy one, but because of the choking gases everything took longer. Time and time again Craig staggered back up the slope to breathe some fresh air, then stumbled back to the helicopter to continue the job. After an hour, he was done.

Nervously, he tried the radio. "Are there any helicopters near the vent?" he asked. "We're in the crater."

"In the crater?" he heard a surprised voice answer. It was the pilot of their back-up helicopter.

"I got through! They're sending help!" Craig shouted. Although he couldn't see his friends clinging to the crater wall, he hoped they could hear him above the roar of the volcano.

––––

From their position high up the crater wall, Michael and Chris could barely see each other, let alone Craig or the helicopter.

Thick haze obscured their view, and poisonous gases stung their eyes and tore at their lungs.

The roar of the volcano blocked sound, too. They couldn't hear Craig shouting from far below. They didn't know that help was on its way.

Craig waited beside the helicopter. The fumes seemed thicker now and as the minutes ticked past, he felt woozy. An hour after placing the call, he heard the sounds of an approaching helicopter.

"I'm to your right," he told the pilot through the radio.

The pilot followed Craig's directions, landing just 10 metres away. Craig ran from the wreck and hurled himself into the rear seat of the helicopter. The clouds were dense, and the pilot soon found himself choking on the fumes. There was no time to look for the others. Gunning the engine, he dodged overhanging rocks and flew the chopper out of the crater.

For Craig, it was a bittersweet moment. He was safe, but his friends were still trapped in the volcano, clutching steep rocks, fighting drifting fumes. At least I know where they are, Craig told himself. I can help the rescuers find them.

Still stranded on the volcano's inner wall, Chris clung to his remote perch while Michael settled on a rocky ledge a dozen metres below. The afternoon wore on, crisscrossed with dashed hopes and rising despair. At one point the men heard the familiar *chop-chop* of a helicopter, but the haze was so thick that they couldn't see a thing, and the sound soon faded.

Later Chris heard shouts from the volcano rim high above. Led by Craig, rescuers had arrived at last. They dangled bright orange ropes over the edge, manoeuvring them back and forth, hoping to somehow reach the trapped men. But visibility was nearly zero and, after hours of trying, the rescue was abandoned.

The sun set, and rainstorms drenched Chris and Michael throughout the long, lonely night. In the morning, they could hear that the rescuers had returned. But the noxious fumes corroded the metal clips on both their climbing ropes and their rescue equipment. Even with gas masks, breathing was difficult. After a short time the rescuers decided they would have to find another way.

In the afternoon Chris decided to take matters into his own hands. It was getting harder and harder to breathe. "I can't sit here any more," he called down to Michael. "I'm going to climb out." For more than twenty-four hours he had been trapped on the rocky shelf. The rescuers gone, his throat raw, the chances of falling ever present, he could not bear the thought of spending another night in this desolate place.

"Stay where you are. It's too dangerous," Michael shouted back.

But Chris wouldn't listen. Already he was on his way, gagging on fumes, finding toeholds wherever he could, grabbing at jagged rocks, slicing his hands and shredding his skin, desperate to climb out and willing to die trying.

━━━

Loneliness overwhelmed Michael. Craig was gone. Chris, too. Michael wondered how much longer he could survive. Acidic fumes burned his lungs and stung his eyes. He was cold and thirsty.

From his narrow perch, he could see only faint shadows through the swirling mist, but suddenly a bulky shape hurtled past him, falling from the rocks above. It was covered in familiar-looking stripes. Chris was wearing a striped shirt, Michael realized with a start. Oh, my God, he thought, it's Chris!

He heard a hollow thud as the object hit the rocks below. "Chris!" he screamed. But his cries went unanswered. It's my fault, Michael told himself. Why didn't I stop him?

━━━

But Chris hadn't fallen. He had fought his way to the rim of the crater. From there he shouted down to Michael, but his words were lost in the roar of the volcano. Rescuers had left a rope as a marker on the ledge, and Chris followed it to the paramedics and rangers who waited on the other side.

Chris told them what he knew. Michael was below, still alive. Unable to climb down because of the poisonous gases, rescuers did the next best thing. They dropped bundles of food, water and clothing over the edge. The packages, a maze of stripes and colours designed to be visible in the fog, bounced down the slope and crashed to the bottom. Their hope was that Michael would notice and be able to reach them — his life depended on it.

———

Inside the crater, night was upon Michael once again as his second day on the rocky ledge drew to a close. He didn't know that Chris was safe, or that rescuers had attempted to help him. All he knew was that he was alone — alone in hell. As the night wore on, he thought of his family. His wife and two children needed him, just as he needed them. Somehow that kept him going. He couldn't give up. But it was getting harder to breathe. By morning, his throat was raw. He couldn't yell for help any more, and as the day wore on he began to lose hope.

Suddenly he heard a helicopter. It sounded close, and through a break in the swirling mist he spotted the tell-tale shape of a chopper above him. He waved frantically. The pilot waved back. "We're lowering a rescue net," a voice boomed over the helicopter's speaker system.

Michael reached into the fog, blindly waving his arms, hoping to catch the edge of the net. After a few futile attempts he grabbed something solid, pulled the net close and dived into it.

He was safe, and so were his companions. They had all survived, beating tremendous odds. To Michael, it was a clear victory.

"I won. You lost," he shouted to Kilauea as he left.

DON'T GIVE UP!

Matt Sanders huddled in his sleeping bag, fighting the fierce cold and piercing wind. He was alone, trapped on a mountain in the middle of one of the worst winter storms in a century.

Matt Sanders awoke to the howling wind, "a noise so loud it sounded like a jet," he'd say later. The wind whipped across the Swiss Alps, driving fresh snow into a frenzy. Visibility was nearly zero, the air thick and white. The trail that Matt had followed just the day before was gone, buried under impossibly deep drifts. It was cold, so cold. Icy fingers crept along his spine, sucking the heat right out of his body. He drew the sleeping bag closer, hugging it tight. There was nothing else he could do. Just wait it out.

It was December 25, 1999 — Christmas morning. But for the twenty-three-year-old American university student, there was little reason for celebration. He was curled up under a rocky ledge on one of Switzerland's most rugged and deadly mountains, caught in one of the worst storms to hit Europe in a hundred years.

Matt had left his hotel room in the Swiss town of Zermatt early the previous morning, aiming to make a one-day hike to a gondola station on the mountain. Forecasters had predicted a winter storm would arrive in a few days, but Matt was confident he could squeeze in one last hike before conditions turned sour. He was an experienced hiker, well-versed in outdoor ways. As an added precaution, he dressed in warm layers, packed a thick sleeping bag, and carried extra food in his backpack. Before he left, he informed hotel staff of his plans. He'd be back later that day, he told them.

The hike took longer than expected. "My biggest mistake was to overestimate my abilities to get through the snow quickly," he said later. "I didn't make it as far as I hoped."

By the time darkness fell over the mountain, Matt was still far from his destination. Rather than risk going on in the dark, he unrolled his sleeping bag under a rocky overhang and hunkered down for the night. While he slept, the wind shifted, grew in strength and tore across the mountain, carrying fresh snow with it.

By morning, the wind was gusting at 200 kilometres per hour. Temperatures had plunged to -30°C, and Matt could barely see a metre or two ahead. To leave now meant certain death, so he did the only thing he could. He curled up in his sleeping bag. He'd wait it out.

The hotel staff knew of his whereabouts, Matt remembered. Someone would notice he was missing and send help. But as conditions worsened and the hours dragged by, he knew that no one would be searching for him. Not yet, anyway. They would be fools to risk their lives in such a storm.

In the town of Zermatt, rescue crews had gathered. Matt hadn't returned, and chances were slim that he would survive alone on the mountain for long. A helicopter was dispatched, but the storm was too high on the mountain, the winds too brisk and unpredictable. The chopper soon returned. There was nothing anyone could do. Just wait, and hope.

Someone called Matt's mother. Your son is missing, she was told. Maybe we'll find him in a day or two. Maybe.

Matt's sleeping bag was thick, one of the best on the market, but by the end of the first day his feet were prickling with pain. He tore into a food package, nibbled on trail mix and tried to conserve his body heat. He focussed on the positive to keep his spirits up. He was alive. He had food. Someone would be coming.

The storm raged on for a second day. On the third, the wind dropped to 160 kilometres per hour, but the temperature continued its steady decline. Matt was out of food now, and his feet were as cold and heavy as blocks of ice. Were rescue crews on their way? he wondered. Would the rescuers be able

High in the Swiss mountains, blizzards can be deadly

to find him, huddled as he was beneath the rocky ledge?

It dawned on Matt that search helicopters could not see him from above, so he dragged himself out and fought his way 60 metres up the slope. It was a slow and painful process. The feeling in his feet was gone, and the wind sucked the last bit of strength from his body. "It would just destroy you, bring you to your knees," he said.

After a six-hour climb Matt collapsed into the snow. He huddled in his sleeping bag, knowing that time was everything now. The sun was setting, and his fourth day on the mountain was almost upon him.

On the fourth and fifth days, winds dropped slightly. Search parties hiked the trails, retracing Matt's route. Helicopters flew over the mountain, too. Both came up empty-handed. There was no sign of Matt. The young man had vanished, and hope dwindled. There was no possibility for survival in such fierce cold. Disappointed, rescue teams called off the search.

Matt's mother was called and informed of the tragic news. Her son was more than likely dead, she was gently told. No one could have survived for so long on the mountain.

Rescuers decided to wait for spring to resume the search. They would be looking for a body, then, and every bit of evidence would be needed to identify it as Matt's. They had to ask his mother to supply a blood sample — her DNA would help provide the proof they needed when the time came.

Matt's family refused to believe the news. They pleaded with the rescuers: Don't give up. Don't leave him there. Just one more sweep of the mountain.

Won over by the family's faith, the rescuers agreed to one final search.

Matt could hear a helicopter. It had to be close. But he had heard helicopters on other days too. Each of those times, he had stepped into the open, waving frantically, only to be met with disappointment. The pilot hadn't been able to see him through the swirling snow.

This time it might be different, Matt figured. The wind had dropped. It was his last chance. He was out of food, and his feet were frozen. It was his sixth day on the mountain, and he couldn't last much longer.

He hobbled to a clearing and waved wildly. The helicopter veered toward him, dropping slightly, as if taking a closer look. Matt's hopes soared. They've seen me! They've seen me!

"I was so thankful someone had come," Matt said later.

Matt Sanders survived the impossible. He believes his positive thinking played a part in the amazing feat. "It's faith in yourself, confidence in yourself, inner strength that you have to rely on."

But Matt believes that a higher power was at work, too. "I don't think you can go through that without having some sort of spiritual response at all. Of course I did. I felt somebody was looking out for me and taking care of me."

Surviving a Blizzard

In a blizzard, high winds and bitter cold mix with snow, producing a killer storm. On average, more than a hundred Canadians die each year in winter storms — more than hurricanes, tornadoes, floods and lightning combined. Here are ways to protect yourself from blizzard dangers:

• Stay indoors. You can easily lose your way in a blizzard and freeze to death.

• If you must go outdoors in a blizzard, tell others where you are going and dress for the weather. Layer your clothing to create "dead air" space that helps insulate against the cold. Wear a water-repellent hat with a breathable outer layer. A jacket with a hood is ideal, and mittens are warmer than gloves.

• If you must travel in a car, carry an emergency kit containing extra clothing, warning flares, a flashlight, a blanket, a first-aid kit, candles, matches and extra food. Take along a shovel and booster cables. Carry a cell phone if you have one.

• If your car gets stuck in a blizzard, do not wander off. Stay calm and remain in the car. Leave one window slightly open and run the car for about ten minutes every half-hour. Be sure the exhaust pipe is not blocked with snow, which will cause exhaust fumes to leak into the car.

• If you get frostbite, try to protect the frostbitten area by keeping it sheltered and dry. Do not rewarm the affected area until you are rescued. Warming it will make you feel the pain, and may hinder your movement.

TIPS FOR SURVIVAL

CAPSIZED

The rogue wave came from nowhere, toppling the boat and trapping Tony Bullimore under the icy waters of the Southern Ocean.

On January 5, 1997, the Southern Ocean was gripped by a storm, with giant waves rising out of the water like walls of ghostly concrete, steep and grey. Between the waves a fleet of yachts struggled to stay afloat.

One of the yachts was the *Exide Challenger*. Aboard the sleek 18-metre vessel was fifty-six-year-old Tony Bullimore. Like others on the ocean that day, he was a contestant in the Vendee Globe, a gruelling solo non-stop race around the world. He rode the waves with steely determination. He was out to win.

Tony was an experienced sailor. He had twenty-seven Atlantic crossings under his belt and he knew the ocean better than anyone else in the race. But the Southern Ocean can be unpredictable. It lies between Australia and Antarctica, a place where waters from three different oceans meet and collide. Here, storms swell out of nowhere, churning the icy water into fury in a heartbeat.

The storm that day was one of the worst, and it took all of Tony's skill to steer the *Exide Challenger*. He was especially wary of rogue waves, unpredictable mountains of water, some the size of eight-storey buildings. If struck broadside by one of these monsters, the *Exide Challenger* could be reduced to splinters in an instant.

After hours of jaw-clenching sailing, Tony took advantage of a break in the storm to go inside the cabin. He closed the hatches securely to prevent water from entering, then settled down for a cup of steaming coffee. Suddenly a loud crack shook the *Exide Challenger*. To Tony, it sounded like the *pow* of a starting pistol being fired into his ear. Before he could act, the boat took a sudden twist and rolled over. "It wasn't a slow capsize," Tony said later. "The boat turned over at a million miles an hour." In no time the boat was upside down, its mast pointed toward the ocean bottom, its keel broken and disabled.

Come on, come on, get upright, Tony begged. But with its keel missing, the *Exide Challenger* was crippled. It remained upside down.

Inside the cabin it was dark, but dry. Tony stood on the cabin ceiling — now the floor — trying to stay upright. It was a tricky balancing act. As waves crashed over the hull the boat bounced wildly, pitching Tony from one side to the other.

The life raft was stowed in the aft end of the craft, on the other side of a main companionway hatch. Tony unlatched the hatch, opening the door and releasing a torrent of water. The force was so great that it severed the tip of his little finger. Despite the pain, he hung on with all his might.

Then disaster struck again. A sudden wave, stronger than many others, shook the boat, sending the boom swinging. It crashed through a window, spilling tonnes of water into the cabin. In the darkness Tony scrambled to find his waterproof survival suit. Without it he'd soon be too chilled to act, too cold to think clearly. He struggled into it.

Tony reviewed his options, but in the end decided he had none. To leave the cabin and swim to the surface to face the storm would be fatal. It was better to ride it out inside the cabin, where it was relatively warm.

Water continued to rise inside the cabin. At first it seemed as if Tony might drown. Then, as pressures evened, the water stopped flowing. At one end of the cabin, the water was up to his chest. Closer to the forward section, though, it was only up to his knees.

Tony realized that no one knew of his predicament, any more than he knew what had happened to the other yachts. He activated his distress beacon and pushed it outside the broken window on a long rope, hoping it would make its way to the surface and transmit a signal.

He prepared for a long wait. He found a narrow storage

compartment with doors and shelves in the forward section. He crawled inside, curled up on the bottom of what had once been the lowest shelf, and fitted a piece of netting around himself to keep from falling out. Here at least he was out of the water. For once, he was grateful for his compact frame.

Time passed slowly. To keep himself occupied, Tony worked out a routine. He regularly sloshed through the water to check the cabin for leaks. He also rigged up a pump to convert salty ocean water to fresh drinking water. He rested a great deal, too, and slept in the tight-fitting storage compartment.

Days rolled by. Every morning a bit of light filtered into the cabin, and Tony realized that daylight had arrived. When it dimmed and the cabin was left in pitch blackness, he knew it was night again. Meanwhile the storm continued to rage, with Tony hanging on to the hope that a search party was on its way. Surely by now someone would have noticed that he was missing.

By the fourth day the cold was beginning to take its toll. Tony felt sluggish. His body was slowing down and his mind was becoming cloudy with confusion — both symptoms of hypothermia. He tried to stay out of the water as much as possible, but water seeped steadily into the cabin, inching ever higher. The yacht was slowly sinking.

On the fifth day the water in the forward compartment was up to his chest. Cold crept through his survival suit, and Tony felt chilled through and through. All at once, above the noise of the turbulent sea, he thought he heard another sound, a whirring *chop-chop* that seemed familiar. Helicopters! he thought. Rescue.

Tony's own words capture the moment. "By now I'm up to my chest in water inside the boat, being sloshed around like a ping-pong ball in a washing machine. The next thing I heard was this *bang, bang, bang* on the side of the hull, and I tell you what . . . that was the greatest, greatest feeling that came into my body . . . I said to myself, 'There is someone out there.'"

Then he heard a deep voice calling him. Excited and

relieved, he pounded on the hull in return. He could wait no longer. Taking a great breath, he dived under the hull and swam to the surface, popping up near an Australian rescue team aboard an inflatable raft.

"It's a miracle," Tony told his rescuers. Indeed it was. Tony Bullimore survived what few others could — eighty-nine hours, huddled in a cupboard, in a slowly sinking boat under the icy waters of what some call the world's most turbulent ocean.

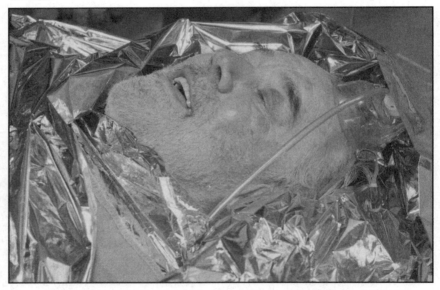

Tony Bullimore in a thermal blanket aboard the HMAS Adelaide

TRAPPED OFF HIGHWAY 97

Joe Spring was trapped inside his crumpled car, hidden from view by dense brush. Without food or water, how many days could he last?

Joe Spring takes a deep breath as he prepares to tell his story. He speaks slowly, softly, as if each word uttered is a small battle won.

It's a short story. Joe remembers packing the car. He remembers saying goodbye before tearing down the highway in his sporty red Nissan. Somewhere, about a hundred kilometres into his journey, though, his memory fades, then stalls completely. It's like he has driven into nothingness. He has no memory of the accident, just a vague recollection of shapes and shadows, and the feeling of helplessness that amnesia brings.

Doctors tell him that someday, his memory will likely return. In the meantime, Joe relies on family, friends, news clippings and the imagination of others to fill the gaps of his story.

On May 21, 2001, Joe Spring left his job at the Safeway store near his home in Aldergrove, B.C. It was already late on that Monday night — around 11 p.m. — when the lanky nineteen-year-old wheeled out of the parking lot and headed east down the TransCanada Highway. He'd packed lightly — a few clothes, a sleeping bag, a box of mini doughnuts, a bottle of drinking water. He had just the bare necessities, enough to get him to his friend's place in Quesnel, a town six hours away. He planned on spending the night there, resting up before continuing on his way to Prince Rupert the next day to attend another friend's graduation.

Near the town of Hope, Joe turned off the TransCanada and headed north along Highway 97. The highway skirted high above the Fraser Canyon, winding its way past thick forests and steep ravines. During the day, the road was busy with traffic. That night it was mostly deserted. The Nissan's headlights pierced the darkness like giant flashlights, illuminating the road a hundred metres ahead. The car ate up the pavement, hugging curves and swallowing hairpin turns with ease.

Joe made good time. Then around 4 a.m., just forty-five minutes from Quesnel, on a straight and ordinary stretch of road, something happened. Perhaps Joe nodded off to sleep for just a second. No one, least of all Joe, knows for sure. But something terrible did happen.

The car suddenly veered and plunged off the road. It crashed against rocks, hit trees, sailed over bushes, tumbled, and broke apart, pitching pieces of itself into the brush. Twenty-five metres down the slope the car smashed to a stop. The windshield shattered and Joe's head hit the steering column. The driver side of the car crumpled around him, and the dashboard collapsed, pinning his legs.

The bushes closed behind the car like curtains closing on a play. From the highway, the car was invisible, hidden by thick brush. No one could see Joe. No one would even know that he was there.

Two days passed before Tim and Teresa Spring began to worry about their son. Joe was dependable, usually on time, not one take off on a whim without at least phoning. When Joe didn't call to say he had arrived at Prince Rupert, his parents knew something was wrong.

They contacted Joe's friends. He had never made it to Prince Rupert, they learned. No sign of him in Quesnel either. The realization that Joe was missing set up a blur of activity. The RCMP were contacted. Search parties were organized. Family and friends traced Joe's route, driving sections of Highway 97, combing the countryside, stopping to ask questions at coffee shops and service stations. Dozens of posters showing Joe and his car were distributed along the way. The *Vancouver Sun* ran the story, and the local television station did a "missing" segment.

A week passed, each day more hopeless than the one

before. There was no sign of Joe, and doubts began to erode his parents' confidence. Without food or water, he might last a few days, five or six at most. Was Joe lying somewhere, broken and battered, still clinging to life, still praying for rescue? Or was he already dead?

———

Joe was alive — barely. His legs and feet were wedged tightly behind the folded wreckage of the car. He could move his arms and head, but the lower half of his body was trapped. The bones in his face were smashed, his left ankle shattered, his ribs cracked, his chest covered in blood and bruises.

Over the days following the accident, temperatures hit highs of 23°C. Insects buzzed around Joe's head, attracted by the blood that oozed from his wounds. At night, temperatures dropped to 2°C. The cold seeped into the car and through Joe's body. His thin T-shirt provided little warmth. The doughnuts were long gone. So was the bottle of water. Joe's throat was parched, his lips swollen and crusted. Hunger gnawed at his stomach.

From his prison in the car, Joe could hear the hum of traffic on the nearby highway. Occasionally he heard the whir of helicopters sweeping overhead. He prayed that someone would notice the car, but no one stopped. Even in his most desperate moments, though, Joe hung on to a single hope — his family. They would still be looking for him. They wouldn't quit no matter what, and neither would he.

The days passed, one folding into the other with incredible slowness. Joe's body was becoming a wasted shadow of its former self. Starved for food and water, it was drawing on its reserves, stripping Joe of muscles, weakening his organs and tissues, sapping him of his last bit of strength.

By the afternoon of the eighth day, death was but a few hours away. Joe drifted in and out of consciousness. He fought to stay alert, hoping against hope that someone might stumble upon him before it was too late. He tried to open his eyes, but through the haze of blood and swollen tissue that was his face, he saw only fleeting shadows. He spotted some movement, two dark shapes lumbering through the brush, edging ever closer to the car. Somewhere in the fogginess of his brain, an alarm bell sounded. Bears!

——

Constable Jodeen Cassidy flew the helicopter with fierce determination. The RCMP pilot skimmed over the forests and ravines that lined Highway 97, looking, always looking, for a glimpse of red amidst the green. It was late afternoon on Tuesday, May 29, eight days since Joe Spring had vanished. The sun was edging closer to the horizon and Constable Cassidy knew that she had time for just one more sweep over the highway before sunset.

Chances were slim that the young man was still alive, but Constable Cassidy had a feeling that this might be her lucky day. She'd had a dream the night before, and in that dream she found Joe. It was a sign she couldn't ignore. Joe was out there somewhere and she would find him.

Beside her, serving as spotter, sat fellow RCMP officer Corporal Al Ramey. It was his day off, and normally he would be busy with other things, but Corporal Ramey felt a strange attachment to Joe, too. Two days earlier, a ragged-looking Tim Spring had stopped at the RCMP detachment in Clinton, B.C. He had pressed a poster into Al's hands, saying, "Our son must be out there." The RCMP officer was struck by the father's anguish, so when Al spotted Jodeen refuelling her helicopter earlier that day, he volunteered to go along.

Jodeen flew the helicopter about 200 metres over the highway's edge. Around 4:45 p.m. she spotted a flash of red. "There it is!"

Al saw it, too, the unmistakable glimmer of steel below. The car was off the highway, nestled among some trees. Al spotted two dark shapes fleeing from the noise of the helicopter, into the forest, one brown and the other black. Bears, he realized. It doesn't look good, he thought.

Jodeen set the helicopter down on a flat rock outcropping. Al leaped out and ran to the wreck, half-expecting to find a mangled body. As he neared the car, he spotted some move-

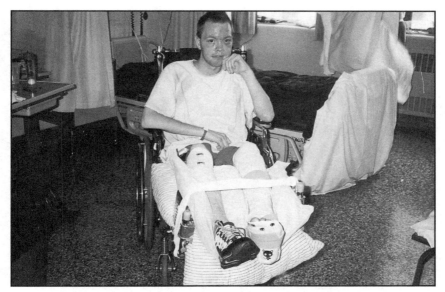

Joe recovering in hospital, and at a physiotherapy session

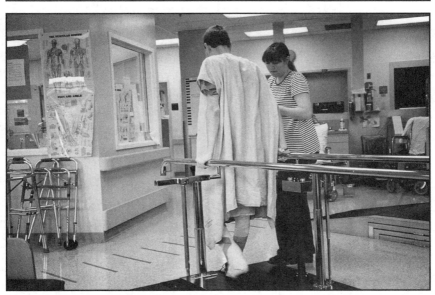

ment. A left arm in the car moved ever so slightly, as if attempting a half-hearted wave.

Joe was still in his seat belt, his body pitched forward over the steering wheel, his right arm in his lap, his eyes swollen

Joe seated in the mangled wreck of his car

shut. A bloodied T-shirt lay outside the car, thrown there perhaps by Joe when he tried to flag down one of the helicopters.

Al reached into the car and put his hand on Joe's shoulder. "It's the RCMP. We've found you," he said simply.

Paramedics arrived in minutes. It took an hour to cut Joe free. He was whisked away to Cariboo Memorial Hospital in William's Lake, then airlifted to Vancouver General Hospital where doctors fed him liquids, operated on his broken body and monitored his fragile state around the clock.

Within weeks Joe was up and about, hobbling down hospital halls, talking to reporters and friends. A month later he was home, enduring painful rounds of physiotherapy and following a strict diet to recover some of the 15 kilograms of weight he had lost during his ordeal.

Joe knows it's only a matter of time before his body returns to its former shape. Just when and how his memories will return, however, is a matter for speculation. Likely they'll come back in foggy waves, glimmers of jumbled images and unsettling flashbacks. Already, he has experienced some of this. When he strains to think about the accident, he has a hazy recollection of dark shadows moving near the crumpled car. Bears, he thinks.

In the meantime, until his mind clears, Joe relies upon others to tell his story. And each day he reminds himself that he has been lucky, very lucky indeed.

"I am alive," he says finally. And for now that is enough for Joe Spring.

Staying Alert Behind the Wheel

Tiredness is a serious threat to road safety. Being drowsy impairs judgment and slows reactions. Here are a few tips to help drivers stay safe behind the wheel:

TIPS FOR SURVIVAL

• When driving, schedule regular stops, at least every two hours.

• Never drink and drive, and avoid medications that make you drowsy.

• If your body tells you that you're tired, stop driving and get some sleep before proceeding.

• Take someone with you on long trips. Passengers can talk with you, keeping your mind alert. They can also share the driving when you need to rest.

• Understand your own biological clock. Everyone has cycles of alertness and drowsiness throughout the day. Once you know your personal cycle, take extra precautions when you are most likely to feel sleepy.

• Avoid driving between midnight and 6 a.m. Statistics show that more accidents due to drowsiness occur at these times than any others.

LOST IN A MAZE

Gustavo Badillo swam from one tunnel to another. He was lost, and time was running out.

On the evening of Saturday, July 13, 1991, Gustavo Badillo and his friend, Eduardo Wallis, donned scuba-diving gear and plunged into the murky water of a subterranean cave in Venezuela. Rumour had it that a network of tunnels deep within the cave led to a mysterious underwater lake, perhaps the largest in all of South America. The two young divers were determined to be the first to find it.

Eduardo carried a sketch of the tunnel system, an incomplete map drawn by British divers years earlier. The map showed small tunnels, branching off the main one like arms extended on an octopus. The pair turned to swim down a narrow corridor, Eduardo leading the way, his air tanks clanging against the rocky overhang.

The cold water was choked with sediment and, even though the men carried lights, visibility was nearly zero. Each kick of Eduardo's fins stirred the black silt, making it even more difficult for Gustavo to see. In his hands Gustavo carried a coil of rope, and as he swam he paid it out bit by bit. One end of the rope was tied to a rock at the cave entrance. To find their way back, they would follow the trail of rope.

The tunnel they had followed led to a small domed chamber, a pocket of air deep inside the mountain. They surfaced to check the map. The tunnel wasn't marked on it. They wondered how many other tunnels were missing on the map.

Thank goodness we have this to follow, Gustavo thought as he pulled on the rope. But the rope felt limp and useless in his hands. Somehow it had become untied.

The two men talked, anxious to come up with a plan. The map could not be trusted, they decided. It wasn't safe to go further. Instead they decided to swim back to the entrance, retie the rope, and try again.

They submerged, Eduardo again leading the way. Stirred by their movements, the water was cloudier than ever. Gustavo soon lost sight of Eduardo. He felt his way along the tunnel, trying to keep up, slamming into rocks here, slipping through crevices there, swimming from one passage to another. Soon Gustavo was dizzy with confusion and overwhelmed by panic. Where was he? Where was Eduardo?

Eduardo swam from tunnel to tunnel. All of them looked alike, and he had the feeling that he had visited some of them before. At last he squeezed through a small opening and surfaced in a large cavern. There Eduardo spotted a flickering light, a candle the men had set in a jar at the entrance, earlier, to mark the spot. He had reached the cave opening. He was safe.

But where was Gustavo? Eduardo expected Gustavo to pop up behind him, but he was nowhere to be seen.

The passages seemed to be getting narrower. Gustavo felt the rock walls closing in on him. Fear crawled along his spine, but he shook it off. I'll need a cool head to stay alive, he told himself.

He surfaced in a small air pocket. There was just enough room for his head, just enough stale air for a quick gulp or two. Gustavo knew there were many small caves like this. How would he know which ones he had visited already? He scraped away slime and muck off the cave roof, leaving a whitened X on the ceiling. That would be his mark. That was how he'd tell.

Eduardo waited for his friend. After forty-five minutes he began to fear the worst. Gustavo would be running out of air. He would be chilled, too, and would soon be fighting hypothermia. I have to do something to save my friend, Eduardo told himself.

Their dive line was lost somewhere under the murky water. Perhaps he could make another. He tied bits of clothing and short pieces of rope together into a makeshift lifeline, tied that securely to a rock and swam back into the maze of tunnels.

Eventually he surfaced in the chamber where he had last seen Gustavo. It was empty. He called out and banged on his tank, hoping for an answer. Hollow silence was his only reply. Eduardo had no choice but to tie the line to a rock, and follow it back to the entrance. He had done all he could. Now it was time to get the help of others.

Inside yet another cavern, Gustavo bobbed to the surface. How many had he entered now? Sixteen, he decided. He scrawled an X on the rocky face — sixteen X's to mark his progress, sixteen different chambers. Not one of them resembled the entrance cave.

He dived again. This time he noticed a current, the tug of running water. He followed it to a chamber larger than any other. It had a small mud island in the centre. At last, a place to rest, a place to breathe.

At daybreak Eduardo drove down the mountain to the nearest village. From the first phone he could find, he called Fernando Indriago, Gustavo's boss at the dive shop where he worked. Words tumbled from his mouth. Gustavo lost . . . eleven hours now . . . underwater. Before hanging up, Fernando calmed the distressed Eduardo as best he could. "I'll get help," he told him. "Don't worry. We'll find Gustavo."

But in his heart, Fernando was not so confident. Finding Gustavo alive after so many hours would be unlikely, even impossible. At best they might find his body wedged inside a tunnel.

Fernando picked up the phone and placed a call. He knew someone who might do the job.

Gustavo sat on his mud island, wrapped in darkness, surrounded by silence. Cold pierced his wetsuit. He shivered uncontrollably. Now and then he called for help and pounded his air tanks with a diving knife. Someone, please hear me, he prayed.

Hours crept by. How long had he been lost? Gustavo fumbled for his watch, but in the darkness he couldn't see it. He tried shining his flashlight on it, but the battery was long dead. He used the light from the flash on his camera instead.

Thirty hours? Gustavo couldn't believe it. Had he really been lost that long? He was filled with despair. Anyone attempting a rescue would have given up long ago. He was alone, lost inside a mountain, sitting on an island in the middle of an uncharted lake that no one could locate. Death seemed certain — a long agonizing death.

Gustavo gripped his diving knife. The blade felt cool, its edge razor sharp. For the first time, he thought about taking his own life.

At the cave entrance a quiet scene unfolded. Fernando, Eduardo and friends of Gustavo huddled around two strangers, divers flown in from Florida who were experts in underwater rescue and recovery — Steve Gerrard and John Orlowski.

Steve and John entered the water carrying a reel of line that had been secured to a rock. Weighted with extra air tanks, hoses and regulators, they disappeared quickly. The two men harboured a fear they didn't want the others to know: Gustavo had been missing for a day and a half. They expected to find a bloated body if anything at all.

In the blackness of what he was sure was his tomb, Gustavo held the knife against his skin. A firm stab into his heart was all it would take to end his misery.

But Gustavo could not do it. Faces of family and friends floated out of the darkness. How disappointed they would be to find that he had chosen this path, that he had given up the struggle to survive. He hurled the knife into the water.

Suddenly, he heard bubbles breaking on the water's surface, and light filled the cavern. A voice called his name, then a man rose out of the water, followed by another man. "I thought I had died," Gustavo said later. "I thought they were angels coming to get me."

It was Steve and John. By chance they had stumbled upon Gustavo's cavern. The three men hugged, and slapped each other on the back. Then, while John stayed with Gustavo, Steve swam back to the entrance.

"He's alive. He's okay!" he told the others. Taking a bottle of sugar water, Steve followed the line back to Gustavo. The sugar water provided Gustavo with nourishment, fuelling him with energy for the return swim. Then, sharing air from John's tank, and supported by the two divers, Gustavo swam to the entrance. The waiting crowd went wild with excitement. After thirty-six hours in his underwater tomb, Gustavo had returned to the land of the living.

For days after his ordeal, darkness was Gustavo Badillo's enemy, quiet conversation his friend. He could not turn out the lights at night. Darkness brought back haunting memories of his brush with death. Talking about it seemed to help, however. Somehow, telling the amazing story to others was just what Gustavo needed.

Cave Safety

Caving is exciting, but also dangerous. It's easy to become lost, disoriented or injured in caves, even in ones that are not underwater.

TIPS FOR SURVIVAL

• Never cave unless you first have proper training.

• Cave with at least one partner. Someone should always be nearby to help you in an emergency.

• Always tell someone outside your caving group where you are going and when you will be back. If you become lost, stuck or injured, someone will know where to look for you if you don't arrive back on time.

• Wear warm water-repellent clothing and footwear. Caves are notoriously cold and often wet.

• Carry more than one light source. Check to make sure that batteries are fully charged before you leave. Nothing strikes fear like being caught in the dark underground.

• Carry an emergency supply kit.

FIRE IN ROOM 211

Black smoke swirled under the doors and spilled into the eighth-grade classroom. Ed Glanz could taste it. There was no escape, no corner safe from it, no refuge at all except at the windows.

It has been decades since the fire at Our Lady of the Angels School in Chicago, but for Ed Glanz the memories hang as heavy as thick smoke. December 1, 1958, is a day he cannot forget. Ninety-two students and three teachers died in that fire. Twenty-four of the dead came from Room 211, Ed's class-room.

It was 2:25 p.m. in Room 211 at Our Lady of the Angels School, and the eighth-grade class was deep into English lessons. The door to the classroom opened, and thirteen-year-old Ed Glanz knew something was wrong even before the teacher did. He was one of the students closest to the rear door, one of two doors leading into the classroom. His wooden desk was the second last in a long row that stretched the length of the room.

Blue haze filled the hallway, and the moment the door opened it spilled into the classroom. Three girls entered. They were classmates of Ed's, returning after running an errand for the teacher, Sister Helaine O'Neill. "Sister," one of them said, "There's smoke in the hall."

There was a slight pause, a moment of hesitation, then Sister Helaine took charge. The classroom was on the second floor of the school, right next to a flight of stairs leading to the main floor. Sister Helaine opened the front door, quickly closed it, then checked the rear door and did the same. Ed noticed the haze was thicker and darker now.

No one, certainly not Sister Helaine, knew that a fire had started in a far-off corner of the basement, or that it had been simmering undetected for some time. Had she known, Sister Helaine might have led her class down the stairs at this point. Instead, she ordered students to the four large windows that lined the outside wall.

Ed rushed through the maze of neatly arranged desks to the nearest window. Normally there were over 60 students in Room 211. The room was crowded, the desks arranged in tight formation: six rows, ten or eleven desks to a row. But today some students — the fortunate ones, as it turned out — were away. Two were home sick, and thirteen boys were out of the school, helping with the annual clothing drive.

The children pushed open the windows and jostled for position, all eager for their share of cold winter air. They yelled and waved, hoping someone would hear them. Smoke swirled under the doors, growing heavier with each passing minute. A fit of coughing gripped the class. Ed could taste the smoke now as the acrid stuff fought its way into his lungs. He considered running from the classroom and dashing down the nearby stairs, but he was torn by confusion. Was it safer to stay and wait it out at the windows?

Soon, Ed no longer had a choice. The fire alarm finally sounded, an endless buzzer barely heard above the clamour of confusion in the room. The classroom grew steadily darker and hotter. There were more than a dozen students at Ed's window, and many more at the other three. It was a tight squeeze. Ed tried to move closer, but a wall of bodies blocked his way. There was no escaping the smoke, no corner safe from it, no refuge at all except at the windows.

The red brick school was built in a U-shape, and Room 211 overlooked a narrow courtyard. So did another classroom along the same side. Children hung out of these windows, too, screaming and waving. Some from the other room climbed down to a canopy overhanging an exit door on the first floor, then slid to the ground. A 2-metre iron picket gate guarded the entrance to the courtyard, but the gate was locked and the children could not open it. Anxious to flee, unable to wait, they climbed over and ran.

Firefighters trying to save the burning school

In Room 211, panic replaced calm. Students screamed. They could not reach the canopy, and for them there was no quick escape. Most, like Ed, were at the windows, gasping for fresh air. Sister Helaine was at the front of the room, a handful of students by her side. She offered comfort and prayer, and suggested to some that they climb down a nearby rainpipe.

Fire trucks finally arrived, and soon firemen were bashing the gate with a long ladder. Four, five, six attempts. Then the lock gave way, the gate swung open and a rush of people flooded the courtyard. A few ladders were tossed against the wall, many of them too short to reach the upper windows. Firemen opened safety nets, and pleaded with the children to jump.

Some students climbed up to the window sill. They teetered at the edge, staring down, trying to decide. It was a long way to the ground, 10 or 15 metres. From this height, the safety nets seemed about the size of a dime. Should they jump, risking injury or even death? Some climbed back down — it was too far, too scary. Others leaped, taking their chances. They tumbled out of the window, some landing in safety nets. Many others struck the pavement, fracturing legs and ankles. A few somersaulted, landing on their backs or faces, their heads cracking on the pavement.

It was stiflingly hot in the room. Fifteen minutes, perhaps twenty, had passed since the start of the madness in Room 211. To Ed, it was an eternity. Every second counted now.

One fireman propped a long ladder below Ed's window. Students rushed to the opening, cramming themselves in thick layers against the sill, making it impossible for Ed to move. In a frenzy, those closest to the window grabbed at the ladder, but they were pinned against the ledge by those pushing from behind.

A brawny fireman scaled the ladder and reached into the room. He groped at the opening, trying to loosen the knot of students at the window. Finally he seized one student and yanked him through the window, swinging him around and releasing him once his feet touched the ladder. Then the fireman reached in again and again, saving some, bypassing others, engaged in a fight against time.

Flames shot out of the ventilator grilles and crept across the ceiling. Fiery tiles fell to the floor, igniting papers and books. The heat was so intense that shirts and sweaters started to burn. In a few minutes, the air in the room reached its flash point, and exploded in a thunderous blast. The children at the window disappeared, silenced by the roar of the fire.

—

A dozen or so children from Room 211 were rescued by that one fireman. Many of them, as it turned out, were boys who were wearing belts. Most of the girls were not. The belts provided the fireman with an easy-to-grab handle, and gave the boys at the window an advantage over the girls.

Ed Glanz was one of those rescued before the classroom erupted into flames. "I was at the one window where the ladder was long enough," he explained. "When the fireman first

A burned-out classroom

tried to get me out, too many kids were jammed against me. He tried to pull me out and he couldn't. He let go and pulled someone else, but I held on to him. He had to pull me out."

Free from the classroom, Ed sat for a while on a curb with a friend who'd been helping with the clothing drive. "I remember seeing Sister Helaine being helped by another nun. She still had her black habit on, but was mostly in a state of shock. I later found out that she had . . . severe burns over sixty-five percent of her body. After a short time, I looked back at the window I had gotten out of and saw flames shooting out of it."

Around 4 o'clock, Ed walked home. He remembers his mother's relief as he entered their apartment, the look of worry vanishing the moment she knew he was safe. The rest of the day is a blur, an eerie blend of the real and unreal. Ed had a newspaper route, and he remembers delivering papers later, his mind numb, his bicycle finding its own way down the well-travelled path. He recalls his older brother driving him to a clinic for treatment. He remembers sitting in front of the television set, staying up past midnight to watch news reports of the tragedy, the lists of the dead and injured climbing steadily. Later, Ed recalls, he lay on his bed, unable to sleep, haunted by the faces of friends never to be seen again.

Over the next week, Ed attended wakes and funerals. There were so many dead that services had to be held in shifts, often in halls and churches far across town. One wake was for ten or twelve children, and even today Ed can still see the caskets, some in the chapel of the funeral home, others lined up in aisles, too many for any one room to hold.

Ed Glanz knows he was incredibly lucky. Other than smoke inhalation, he escaped the fire unscathed. Many other children suffered burns, broken bones, and disfigurement. Survival in any form carries a price, however. "You kind of look back on it as you get older, and that's when it affects you. You start to realize the impact that this had on people's lives."

For most survivors, it's the feelings and memories that are hardest to resolve. Ed remembers a phone call he had with another survivor of the fire. "I was talking to this fellow, when suddenly it hit us. We both started crying, and that was thirty years after the fire."

Every once in a while Ed gathers with other survivors of the fire. They talk, share memories, renew contacts. They've grown closer over the years, and many of them keep in touch by phone and e-mail. It's their way of handling the tragedy, a way of answering questions that have no answers.

Tragic as it was, the fire had at least one positive result. It sparked reforms in many schools around the world. New safety regulations and stricter building codes were enforced to ensure that such a disaster would never happen again.

Escaping Fire

Keep these strategies in mind to survive a house fire:

• Plan at least two ways to escape from every room of your home.

• Practise your escape route with your family at least twice a year.

• Select a place outside your home for everyone to meet.

• If the building is on fire, stoop low or crawl along the floor. Smoke and poisonous gases are less likely to collect there.

• If you are escaping through a closed door, feel the door or door handle before opening it. If it is warm to the touch, a fire may be raging on the other side. Try an alternate route.

• If flames, smoke or heat block your escape, stay in the room with the door closed.

• Place a bright-coloured cloth in the window to signal for help. If there is a phone in the room, or if you have a cell phone, call 911.

• Once you are out, stay out. Call the fire department from a neighbour's house.

TIPS FOR SURVIVAL

WEDGED IN ROCK

Paul Hartness was wedged in the narrow crevice, his arms pinned above him, his chest squeezed between the rocks. No amount of pulling could set him free.

Tuesday, August 26, 1997, was a scorcher. Temperatures soared to 40°C in the desert near Palmdale, California, a suburb of Los Angeles. But the heat didn't stop eleven-year-old Paul Hartness and his friend, Rodney Kundel, from romping over the rocky hills behind the Kundel home. It was a glorious day, perfect for carefree adventures.

A little after noon, when the sun was at its blazing highest, Paul scaled a 9-metre-high boulder. Rodney had already completed the climb, and Paul was anxious to prove he could do it, too. The boulder rose like a giant egg above the other rocks. It was smooth and blistering hot. A crevice ran like a jagged lightning bolt through the boulder, splitting it in two from top to bottom.

Partway up, Paul lost his balance and slipped. He fell feet-first into the crevice, plummeting several metres, then stopping suddenly as the rock caught him. He hung suspended, his chest held in a vise-like grip by the rock, his feet dangling below, his arms pinned above.

Paul tried to free himself. Rodney tried, too, yanking on Paul's arms, hoping to pull him sideways just enough to dislodge him. But the more Paul moved, the more he slipped into the narrow chasm.

Rodney ran for help, telling Paul he would be back as soon as he could. Paul pressed against the rock, hoping to relieve some of the force on his chest. His ribs felt like they were about to collapse. There was no space for his chest to expand, and each breath was painfully difficult.

Rodney finally returned, bringing rescuers from the Los Angeles County Fire Department. They attached straps to

Paul's wrist and tried pulling him sideways toward a wider part of the crevice. But he was firmly wedged in the rock, and the tugging only caused him more pain. He screamed for them to stop.

The rocks were sizzling hot, and the unforgiving sun beat down on Paul's head. One of the rescuers slipped a hat onto him, giving him a small measure of shade, but still he felt woozy. He was running out of air, slowly strangling, and each breath, each wiggle or tug, only forced him deeper and tighter into the crevice.

Desperate to keep Paul from slipping any further, rescuers shoved rocks, ladders and pieces of wood under his feet to stabilize him. A pulley system was mounted on top of the boulder. Ropes were tied to Paul, but no amount of heaving budged him.

Time was precious now. Paul's condition was rapidly deteriorating. Bystanders talked to him, hoping to keep him alert, but he drifted in and out of consciousness. He was edging dangerously close to death. If he dropped even a few more centimetres, his chest would be so compressed that it would be impossible for him to draw a breath.

Then someone came up with a wild plan. Why not pour cooking oil over the boy? Maybe if they lubricated his whole body he would slip out from the rocks when pulled.

The plan had its share of risks. Under the desert sun, the rocks were close to 50°C, hot enough to heat the oil to a dangerous temperature. If the plan didn't work, if Paul couldn't be hauled out of the crevice in just a few minutes, he could very well fry to death.

Corn oil was poured over the boy and slathered on the rocks around him. Then rescuers pulled again. "Stop. Please stop," Paul pleaded. He felt like he was being torn in two. But the rescuers ignored his cries. This was Paul's last chance, and they had only a short time to free him. Under the relentless pulling Paul moved slowly, a centimetre at first, then another. As his chest cleared the rocks, he slipped faster, almost popping out of the cavity.

He was carried by stretcher to a waiting ambulance. As he passed the crowd of onlookers who had gathered around the rock, he flashed a smile. "I was scared, but now I'm fine," he told them.

Other than a few cuts and rope burns, Paul survived the ordeal intact. Although he still romps around the rocky hills, he is much more cautious. He realizes how close he came to death. "I'm so glad to be alive," he says.

SWALLOWED ALIVE

Alone on the beach, up to his waist in quicksand, Tony Howlett knew that the tide was returning, and every minute counted.

Terry Howlett tried not to panic. He was sinking — surely, steadily. In a matter of seconds, the sand was past his ankles, and the more he struggled the faster he sank.

On that August night in 1996, the sky was clear, the moon bright and full. Twenty-nine-year-old Terry had gone for a walk along the shoreline of Morecambe Bay in northwest England that Saturday evening. When he came to a wide river channel that cut across the beach, he decided to cross. The tide was out and the exposed river bed was a rippling plain of sand spotted with reeds and glistening tidal pools. Terry figured it was a safe place to walk. But he was wrong, dead wrong.

Terry had taken only a dozen steps when he began to sink. He waved his arms to keep his balance, but the movement just made him sink faster. Before long he was up to his knees in quicksand.

I should lie down, spread my weight and try to float on the sand, Terry thought. But already it was too late for that. He was firmly wedged in an upright position. He tried standing still, hoping that would stop the pull of the sand. But it didn't. The quicksand sucked him down, oozing past his knees, then climbing up his thighs.

Terry's imagination ran wild. He pictured himself disappearing into the sand, vanishing without a trace. He could almost feel the sand seeping into his nose and throat, sucking the very life from his body. I'm being swallowed alive, he thought.

As the sand reached his waist, the sinking stopped just as suddenly as it had started.

For a moment Terry breathed easier. Then the seriousness

of his situation hit home. He was locked in sand, alone on a desolate beach in the middle of the night, far from anyone who might help him. Worst of all, there was the tide. When Terry had started his walk, the tide had been going out. That meant it would return in the morning, engulfing everything — and everyone — on the river bed.

Using his hands as shovels, Terry tried digging himself out of the muck, but each scoop of sand slipped back into place. After an hour Terry's arms were sore, his legs tight with cramps, and he was no closer to being free. Still, what else could he do?

Throughout the long, lonely night, Terry scratched at the sand. Now and then he called out for help, but he knew that no one could hear him. Everyone was indoors or too far away. Moving the heavy wet sand sapped his strength. He grew tired, but Terry knew he couldn't give up. As long as he could move even a bit, there was a tiny measure of hope.

By morning Terry was exhausted. He was grateful for the warmth of the rising sun, but daylight also renewed his fear of the tide. Soon it would return, and there seemed to be nothing more he could do to save himself.

Suddenly it dawned on him that others might now be outside enjoying the sunshine. Perhaps if he shouted again someone might hear him. "Help me," he called. "Help me." His voice rolled over the desolate sand. There was no one in sight, no one to hear his desperate cries.

An hour passed, then another. Terry craned his neck, looking toward the sea, half-expecting the tide to return at any moment. He kept calling until his voice grew hoarse, hoping that someone — a jogger, a sheep herder, a fisherman, anyone who happened to be nearby — would hear him.

Just when things seemed their bleakest, Terry heard a distant voice.

"Where are you?" it called.

"Over here," Terry yelled back.

Across the river bed, he spotted three people racing toward him. They had heard his cries echoing over the barren

Rescuers moving Terry Howlett to the beach just before the tide reaches him

shoreline and had been searching for him since sunrise. One of them, a police officer, went to radio for help while the other two men tried pulling Terry out of the sand, which had dried out and become firmer. Terry screamed in pain. He was wedged in tightly.

Emergency crews soon arrived and before long the shoreline was crawling with firefighters, paramedics and rescue equipment. In the back of everyone's mind was the incoming tide. It was now 7:30 a.m. and, if calculations were correct, the tide was due at 8:38 a.m. There was no time to lose.

Hastily the rescuers reviewed the options. Pulling Terry out was impossible, as he was firmly cemented into the sand. Bringing in a mechanical digger was pointless, too. With its tremendous weight, the machine would only sink into the sand. Someone suggested adding compressed air to the sand, thinking that it might loosen the sand's hold on Terry. But when firefighters tried blasting air into the sand, they found it only made the sand harder.

Rescuers could now see a wavering glimmer near the

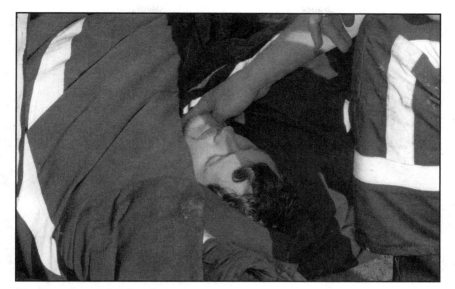

Terry safe on dry land

mouth of the channel. The tide was coming. Soon water would be gushing around their ankles. Working feverishly, they tried something new. Pipes and hoses from the fire trucks were lugged across the beach and a steel tube was jammed into the sand near Terry. Using water under high pressure, they blasted at the muck around him.

The tide moved quickly, rising 5 centimetres a minute. Water was soon lapping at the rescuers' ankles, softening the sand and sucking them down. Again and again, they had to pull each other out of the gooey mess.

Soon the water was swirling under Terry's chin, and he was minutes from death. It was becoming more dangerous for the rescuers, too. There was talk of supplying Terry with a face mask and piping in air to give him a few extra minutes. But there was also whispered talk of pulling out, of abandoning the rescue, and heading for the safety of the shore.

Just then one of the men pushed the high-pressure nozzle down the side of Terry's leg. The blast of water pushed the sand aside, freeing his right leg. Cheers erupted. Locking their arms under Terry, the rescuers pulled, yanking him free.

Terry was rushed up the beach just as the tide — more than a metre deep now — rushed in and filled the spot where he had been trapped. He spent a day in the hospital. Except for a bout of hypothermia, he survived the experience, grateful for a second chance at life.

Surviving Quicksand

Quicksand forms when moving water surrounds sand grains and saturates the spaces between. It acts more like a liquid than a solid. If you are stuck in quicksand, try to follow these tips:

TIPS FOR SURVIVAL

• Stay calm. Rapid movements will only cause you to sink deeper.

• If the sand is deep, lie on your back. Spread your arms and legs far apart. This will distribute your weight evenly and help you float. In this position, you might be able to lift one leg at a time out of the sand.

• Rest often. Take deep breaths, keep your lungs filled with air, lie back and relax to regain your strength.

CLOUD OF DEATH

The tanker car hurtled through the air, skidded across the ground, then slammed into the house, spewing clouds of poisonous gas into the air and trapping the Wieland family inside.

Friday, January 18, 2002, started off normally enough. Most of Minot, North Dakota, slept, unaware of the train that rumbled down the Soo Line, the rail line that cut across the middle of town. Just past midnight the train derailed, buckling like a wounded snake, rail cars snapping their couplings, metal shooting everywhere, fire erupting in a thunderous blast. One rail car, a tanker filled with dangerous anhydrous ammonia, hurtled 7 or 8 metres into the air, hopped over a dike, sliced through a grove of trees, then skidded across a field like a runaway iron beast. It missed one house and another, then plowed into a third, carving a hole into its side. Flames sprayed the sky and a cloud of poisonous gas billowed over the town.

The night was normal no longer.

Seventeen-year-old Jake Wieland awoke with a start. Somewhere in the far reaches of his sleepy mind, he thought he had heard an explosion. The house was pitch black, darker than on most nights, it seemed. A pungent odour wafted into Jake's room. His telephone started beeping, a clear sign that the power was out. From down the hall, he could hear footsteps and excited voices. His parents, Lee and Carmel, were up. Something was wrong.

"Get some clothes on. We have to leave," he heard his father call.

Jake stumbled into the living room. His parents had been thrown out of bed, their bedroom windows shattered, glass firing like bullets across the room. There had been an explosion for sure, but just where and why no one knew for certain.

Lee found a flashlight and led the family to an outside

door. The smell outside was overpowering, the air milky white — "thicker than the thickest fog you've ever seen," Lee would say later. He had worked on farms much of his life, and he recognized the odour. It was anhydrous ammonia, a toxic liquid fertilizer.

Run, instinct told him. Run for your life. But Lee resisted the impulse to flee. He slammed the door closed. Exposure to anhydrous ammonia could cause burns, irritation to the respiratory system, even death. They couldn't escape outside. At best they might take a few steps before the gas overcame them. Their only option was to wait indoors.

Poisonous fumes were already seeping into the Wielands' house, saturating the air, making their eyes water, their throats burn. Was there any place safe? Any pocket of fresh air, or a corner of the house free from the noxious gas?

They tried the basement, but the smell was strong there, too. As a last resort they headed to the unheated garage attached to the house, climbed a few stairs and crawled into a small attic space above. The smell of ammonia there was weaker.

It was cold in the attic, though. January cold. It was the dead-of-winter kind of cold that robs the body of heat in an instant. The three of them lay on the floor, huddled under a single sleeping bag, sharing each other's warmth. They had moved into the house just a year before, and Carmel had stored a few boxes of baby clothes in the attic. They fished out the tiny garments, and held them over their faces, hoping to filter out the deadly gas. Then they waited. Someone would come, they hoped.

Hours ticked by. Around 2:30 a.m., Jake heard a phone ring deep within the house. Miraculously, one of the lines still worked. He barrelled down the steps, choking on the fumes, and bolted inside the house. He snapped up the receiver and just caught the caller before he hung up. It was a friend, phoning to check on them after hearing news reports about the explosion. "Get help," Jake pleaded moments before the fumes drove him back to the garage.

The railway car punched a huge hole in the Wieland house

A clothes closet lies exposed after the railway car hit the house

113

The Wielands waited in the attic, hopeful now that someone would soon be on their way. Their rescuers would bring facemasks, and then it would all be over. But as time wore on, as the bitter cold and toxic fumes gnawed at their minds and bodies, and still no one came, Lee ran downstairs again and dialled 911 himself. "Stay where you are," he was told. "Someone will come to get you." No one ever did. In desperation, they tried 911 three more times throughout the night.

At some point, Lee went downstairs and poked his head outdoors. The air was better out there, he reported. They fumbled down the dark stairs, and circled around the house. For the first time they saw the tanker, its end buried deep into their house, a gaping hole right into their bedroom. Later, they would be told that a second chunk of metal had hit the garage, and a third had pierced the bedroom wall. But right now there was no time to investigate or to flee. Another wave of ammonia hit them, and they were forced back upstairs.

Over the next few hours, their situation grew more desperate. Jake's fingers grew numb and his feet tingled from the icy cold. They were alone, the gas as thick as ever, their lungs raw, the cold sapping their strength, hope fading with each passing minute. They prayed for strength, and for each other, not certain that they would live to see the sun rise.

Around 6:30 a.m., they could wait no longer. Lee crept downstairs and called a neighbour. The neighbour told Lee that the gas wasn't as bad at his house. Lee, Jake and Carmel decided to risk it. Quickly they climbed into their car and gunned it to the neighbour's house a short distance away.

An hour later rescue workers reached them and led them to hospital. Their skin was burned. The linings of their lungs and noses were irritated. They spent several hours receiving oxygen. Considering the alternative, though, they were lucky.

"If we had gone out, we would have died," Lee said. Other neighbours had strayed outdoors, only to be overcome by the deadly fumes. One man, who lived only 30 metres from the Wielands, died trying to make a run for it. Another spent weeks in the hospital, crippled from the poison. In all, about 140 people were treated for respiratory problems and other complications.

To Lee and Carmel Wieland, their son is the hero in all of this. "I was really proud of him. He was so grown-up in this situation," Lee said. "His mother got really cold, and he tried to keep her warm. When we were ready to leave, it was pitch dark and she thought she'd never make it down. He wouldn't leave without her."

DAY OF TERROR

From his office window on the eighty-first floor of World Trade Center Tower Two, Stanley Praimnath saw United Air Lines Flight 175 barrelling straight for him.

September 11, 2001, started as just another day for three men at the Twin Towers of the World Trade Center in New York City.

By 8:40 a.m. Michael Hingson, a fifty-one-year-old executive, was already at work on the seventy-eighth floor of Tower One, the North Tower. Michael has been blind from birth. His guide dog, Roselle, lay curled under his desk, sleeping peacefully.

Across the courtyard, on the eighty-fourth floor of Tower Two (the South Tower), Brian Clark was sitting at his desk, his back to the window. For the vice-president of Euro Brokers, it was business as usual.

Three floors below Brian, on the eighty-first floor of the South Tower, Stanley Praimnath was in his office, too. He chatted casually to a secretary, then stood by his desk to retrieve his phone messages. Through the window he could see the North Tower and the Statue of Liberty, tall and proud in the harbour.

At 8:45 a.m. the North Tower exploded into flames. Fireballs shot up to the roof, and glass and concrete cascaded into the street hundreds of metres below. Although none of the three men knew it yet, an airplane had smashed into the North Tower.

A day of terror had begun.

In the North Tower, fifteen floors below where the airplane had struck, Michael Hingson felt and smelled the explosion. "I heard a loud noise like a bump and then a lot of shaking. It was worse than any earthquake I've ever experienced," he said. "The building started swaying, and the air was filled with smoke, fire, paper and the smell of kerosene."

After making sure his co-workers and some visitors were on their way down the stairs and out of the building, Michael put the harness on Roselle. With the help of a co-worker, David Frank, he started making his own way down a stairwell and toward the ground.

Brian Clark, at his desk in the South Tower, heard an enormous thump. The overhead lights buzzed for a moment, then a sudden flash filled the room. He spun around to stare out the window. "The entire airspace behind me was filled with flame," he said. "I didn't know what it was at the time, but it was the fuel from the first jet hitting the North Tower."

Brian had been trained to act as a fire marshal in times of crisis. He grabbed his whistle and flashlight, then spun into action. "Get out! Everybody get out!" he yelled. He glanced out the window again. Thousands of papers were fluttering through the air, their edges all on fire.

A few floors down, Stanley Praimnath and others in his office rushed to the elevator and scooted down to the seventy-eighth-floor interchange, eager to catch elevators that would take them to the ground floor. A security guard stopped them and assured them that there was no reason to panic. "Two World Trade is secured. Go back to your office," Stanley remembered him saying. Employees throughout the building returned to their offices.

Stanley and the others rode the elevator back to the eighty-first floor. His phone was ringing as he stepped into his office. He answered it, calmly telling a concerned caller that there was nothing to worry about. That's when he looked out the window and spotted the horror approaching outside.

"I was looking toward the Statue of Liberty," he recalled, "and in mid-sentence, I said, 'I have got to go. A plane is heading for me.'"

It was United Air Lines Flight 175, on a collision course with the South Tower.

Firefighters inspecting a piece of the wreckage

"I saw this plane eyeball-to-eyeball. It was like the biggest thing I've ever seen coming toward me. But this is all happening in slow motion."

Stanley dropped the phone and took cover under his desk, not a moment too soon. The plane ripped into the side of the building, exploding in a giant fireball of jet fuel and debris. In the span of a single heartbeat, the office disappeared. Windows shattered, walls collapsed and the ceiling crumpled and fell. Flames flickered among heaps of rubble, and smoke as heavy and thick as storm clouds hung in the air.

An interior wall collapsed over Stanley, burying him up to his shoulders. For the most part he was unhurt, but he knew he had to get out fast. He could see the flaming wing of the plane hanging in the doorway of his department, and the stench of jet fuel was overpowering. He tore at the debris, pushing and shoving it aside, but he was hopelessly trapped beneath the wall. He uttered a silent prayer. Then he started yelling for help. Is there anyone left to hear me? he wondered.

In the North Tower, Roselle and David Frank were calmly leading Michael Hingson down the stairs. Roselle had been his faithful guide for years, and Michael needed her help now more than ever.

The smell of jet fuel filled the air, making it hard to breathe. Temperatures were climbing, too. Michael was sweating, and Roselle was panting and thirsty, her throat scratchy from the fumes. She stopped now and then to lap at puddles of water on the floor, puddles created by bursting pipes.

The stairwell became busy with people. They jostled past Michael, sometimes bumping into him. He soon realized that some of them were going the wrong way — up instead of down. "I heard applause and was told that they were firefighters," he said. "I clapped a few on the back, but I was scared for where they were going."

Partway down the stairs, they noticed that the stench of jet fuel was even stronger. What they *didn't* know was that, by then, a plane had also crashed into the other tower.

Brian Clark was back in his office when the plane hit the South Tower several floors below him. The lights went out and there was the sound of a muffled, distant explosion. Ceiling tiles popped loose and the floor seemed to buckle. The entire building twisted and rocked.

"For seven to ten seconds, there was this enormous sway in the building," he recalled later. "It was one way, and I just felt in my heart, 'Oh my gosh, we are going over.' That's what it felt like. . . . I thought it was over."

Just when it seemed that the whole structure would topple, the building moved back into position and righted itself. The office was filled with thick, chalky dust. Fortunately, Brian had his flashlight, and he used it to lead his co-workers to Stairway A, one of several stairways on his floor. As luck would have it, it was the stairway farthest from the point of impact between the seventy-eighth and eighty-first floors.

They started down the stairs, the flashlight's beam piercing the darkness ahead. Around the eighty-first floor they met two people in the stairwell who were coming up. One of them reported too much smoke and flames below. "You can't go down."

A disagreement broke out. Should they go back up, or keep going down? But Brian never heard the end of the discussion. Above their rising voices he heard banging instead, and a remote cry coming from beyond the mangled stairwell door. "Help! Help! I'm buried. I can't breathe. Is anybody there? Can you help me?"

Drawn by the sound, Brian pried back the damaged door, pushed aside the broken wall and squeezed through. He scanned the eighty-first floor with his flashlight. "Who's there? Where are you?" he called.

Through the swirling dust and mounting flames, Stanley Praimnath heard Brian's voice, and spotted the shimmering light. "I see the light. I see the light," he cried.

Brian waved the flashlight, uncertain where the voice was coming from. "No, to the right . . . to the left . . ." Stanley called. Then he stuck his hand through a tiny opening in the debris, and waved it around like a flag. "Can you see my hand?"

Brian spotted it, a hand poking through the ruins. He reached through the rubble, grabbing hunks of plaster and tile, pitching them sideways, trying to get to Stanley. He couldn't. One last barrier remained.

"You've got to jump over," Brian said. Stanley tried, but he fell backwards instead. "Come on, you've *got* to do this," Brian repeated. "It's the only way out."

Stanley jumped again. At the same moment Brian reached to grab him, caught Stanley's collar, and yanked him over.

They fought their way back to the stairwell. Unknown to Brian, the others in his group had climbed back upstairs. Brian and Stanley headed down instead. After all, they figured, it was the upper storeys that were on fire, not the lower ones. The stairs were dark and smoke filled; debris littered the way. The sprinkler system was on, and water sloshed over

Pieces of twisted metal were all that remained of the towers

their feet. The stairs twisted and turned. Mostly empty, they seemed to go forever.

On the thirty-first floor Stanley and Brian stopped in a deserted office to use the phone. Brian called his wife. "I'm okay," he reassured her. "Don't worry." Stanley phoned his wife and told her the same.

The two continued down the remaining stairs. There seemed to be no reason to hurry. When they finally reached the lobby, they met firefighters and emergency rescue teams.

The South Tower was surrounded by debris, and more was falling from the sky. "Run. Run out of the building! Go, go, go!" they were told. They waited until there was a break in the fallout, then they ran. "We ran out of that building arm-in-arm," Stanley recalled. "I was dragging him and he was dragging me."

They ran to Trinity Church, two blocks away. When they reached the gate they turned around to look back at the South

Tower. It was in flames, but still tall and whole. Then, within minutes, the entire thing crumbled like a house of cards, cascading to the ground in a dense cloud of dust and smoke.

"We just stared at it in awe, not realizing what was happening," Brian said, "But then this great tsunami of dust came over the church. Everyone looked up, and, as in a disaster movie, everybody started running."

It took almost an hour for David, Michael and Roselle to get down the stairs of the North Tower. "By the time we reached the bottom, it had become very hard to breathe," Michael said. "We were . . . very hot and tired."

At this point, both buildings were still standing. The surrounding streets were familiar, but filled with hidden dangers. Michael kept his commands to Roselle simple: "Right" or "Left." With David's help they walked away from the burning North Tower, navigating through debris and crowds, and the commotion of fire trucks and ambulances.

They were about two blocks away when the South Tower collapsed. "It sounded like a metal and concrete waterfall," he said. "We started running for the subway."

About twenty minutes later the North Tower collapsed, too. Despite the confusion and the wave of dust, Roselle wound her way through the streets, leading Michael to safety. Because there were no trains running that day, the pair had to stay overnight with a friend. It wasn't until the next day that they could make it home.

Michael Hingson and Roselle

Stanley Praimnath and Brian Clark fought through the billowing dust and worked their way to safety, too. Without each other, neither one figures he would have survived. Just before parting, Stanley handed Brian his business card. "Keep in contact," he said. "I owe you my life."

But Brian Clark thinks *he* owes Stanley Praimnath just as much. "You know, Stanley," he said after the ordeal. "You may think I saved your life, but I think you saved my life, too. You got me out of that argument as to whether I should go up or go down. I'm here, and I'm fine, and it's because of your voice in the darkness that I made it."

Somehow, the tragedy has created an unbreakable bond between strangers.

For Michael Hingson and Roselle, life has not been the same since. Michael has switched jobs and now serves as a National Public Affairs Representative for Guide Dogs for the Blind, the same organization that trained Roselle. Roselle is still his stalwart companion, but she is famous in her own right. Several groups have recognized her determination and faithfulness to her master, and she has been granted honours reserved for only the most exceptional of animals, including Britain's Dickin Medal and America's ACE Award.

IT'S TEARING OFF MY ARM!

The moment Jeffrey Bush stuck his hand into the chute, he knew he'd made a mistake.

The snowblower rumbled and shook as Jeffrey Bush guided it down his neighbour's driveway. About 10 centimetres of snow had fallen overnight, and the morning of April 13, 2001, Jeffrey was busy clearing the driveways of the houses around his Calgary home.

Normally the snowblower chewed through snow like a ravenous dog gulping down food. It could swallow entire drifts, grinding hard snow to powder before firing it up out of the chute. But today the snowblower grumbled and complained. The snow was especially wet and sticky. As it passed through the blower, the slushy stuff collected on the sides of the chute, where it froze into layers of rock-hard ice. More than once Jeffrey had to stop the machine to knock off the ice that plugged up the opening.

Around noon the snowblower choked once again. The blades churned, but no snow shot from the chute. Jeffrey thought of going back to his garage to get a stick or a wrench, a tool of some sort to dislodge the ice. On the spur of the moment he reached into the chute with his left hand instead.

Jeffrey knew immediately that it had been a mistake. "I remember thinking, what a stupid thing to do, sticking my hand down the chute," he said later. He felt a tug as the blades caught his glove and yanked his hand forward, then grinding pressure as they mangled his fingertips. He pulled back, thinking he could somehow free his hand. The blades continued to churn, tugging even harder, sucking his hand even further into the machine.

My arm! he thought. It's tearing off my arm! There seemed to be no way to stop the machine. Relentlessly the blades chewed on, ripping muscle from bone, grinding Jeffrey's fingers to pulp. Then, all at once, the blades clanked to a halt. The motor growled as it urged the blades forward, but something held them fast. Jeffrey realized that it was his wedding ring. It had become wedged between the chute and the blades, jamming the machine and preventing the blades from crushing even more of his hand.

He breathed a silent prayer of thanks. For the moment, his arm — perhaps even his life — had been spared. But the ordeal was far from over. His hand was still clamped in the machine, and no amount of pulling would free it. Jeffrey could see no blood spurting from his mangled fingers, and he felt little pain. The nerves and blood vessels in his fingers were too tightly pinched to allow any of that.

He glanced down the street. No one was in sight. His neighbours were either at work or in their homes having lunch. He yelled for help. Only the muffled sounds of traffic from distant streets answered his call.

Exactly how bad was the situation? Jeffrey wondered. Were his fingers crushed beyond a hope of repair? Or was there even a shred of a chance that they might be saved? Doctors could do wonderful things, he knew, but time was an important factor. The longer he remained locked in the snowblower, the greater the chance of permanent damage to his hand.

Jeffrey called again and again. Still no one heard his cries. Finally, after fifteen minutes, a woman who was canvassing door-to-door down the street spotted him. She reacted quickly and went into a nearby house to call 911. Within minutes, fire trucks, squad cars and an ambulance arrived at the scene.

The rescue team tried pulling Jeffrey free, but the blades held his hand fast. Someone brought a 2-metre iron bar and tried using it like a lever to pry the machine open. Even that failed to unlock the device. Finally, with all other options exhausted, rescuers did the only thing they could. They started dismantling the gear box.

The process was agonizingly slow. Piece by piece, the device was taken apart. As pressure was slowly released from Jeffrey's fingers, blood started flowing from the wound. He was hit by a wave of numbing pain. He was afraid to look at his mangled hand, afraid that the damage would be too great, the wounds too impossible to repair. When he steeled himself and braved a look, he was left queasy. Three of his fingers were crushed.

Freeing Jeffrey took almost forty minutes. By then, he had been locked in the snowblower for over an hour. He was rushed to hospital where he was whisked into surgery. His three middle fingers were broken but salvageable. Doctors inserted pins, reattached the muscle to the bone, then sewed the flesh together. Part of his index finger, however, was mangled beyond repair, so it was amputated.

▬▬

Time heals all, the saying goes. That was certainly true in Jeffrey Bush's case. In a matter of weeks he regained the use of most of his hand. Luck, he knows, was with him that fateful winter day. His wedding ring stopped his hand, perhaps even his arm, from being eaten by the machine. In the end, the ice that he fought so hard to remove from the chute helped save his mashed fingers. By chilling his hand, the ice preserved the tissue, making it possible for doctors to make miraculous repairs on his mangled hand.

Handling Machinery

Snowblowers, lawnmowers and other household machines are useful tools, but they can also be dangerous if mishandled. Each year thousands of people suffer cuts, crushed and broken bones, burns, infections and amputation due to the improper or careless use of these machines. Here are a few tips to keep in mind when using such powerful equipment:

TIPS FOR SURVIVAL

• Before using, read the instruction manual or have a responsible adult who is familiar with the equipment show you how to use it.

• Do not remove safety devices, shields or guards from the machine. They are there to protect you.

• Before starting up the machine, remove all foreign objects from its path. Metal, stones and bits of wood can become deadly projectiles when snagged by the churning blades of a snowblower or lawnmower.

• Be sure the motor is turned off before inspecting the machine. If a snowblower becomes jammed, shut it off, disengage the clutch and wait more than 5 seconds for the blade to stop rotating.

• Keep hands and feet away from moving parts. Use a stick or broom handle — NOT hands or feet — to remove debris in lawnmowers or snowblowers, only after the machine has been turned off.

• Do not leave a running lawnmower or snowblower unattended. If you must leave the machine, shut off the engine.

TIPS FOR SURVIVAL

IN A FLASH

Lightning leaped from the metal workbench to the thermostat in Christine Fram's hand.

Lightning streaked across Vancouver's sky, not once or twice, but more than 2000 times on the morning of August 6, 1997. Rain fell in sheets, and thunder as loud as cannon fire rocked the city. Inside an automotive shop, twenty-eight-year-old Christine Fram, an apprentice auto mechanic, shuddered with each explosion of light and sound. The storm made her nervous and she found it hard to concentrate on her job.

It's just a summer storm, she told herself. Nothing to worry about. She forced herself back to her work repairing the cooling system of a car. She was using a vise on a metal workbench in a corner of the shop that housed the building's circuit breakers. In her gloved hand she held an aluminum thermostat.

Christine had just stepped back from the bench when a spectacular boom shook the building. A flash of blue light leaped from the metal workbench to the thermostat in Christine's hand, and a jolt of paralyzing pain shot through her arm.

For an instant, time seemed to stand still. Christine stood stunned, rooted to the spot, her rubber glove smouldering. The surge had blown the tips of her glove off, leaving her fingers exposed. They were raw, blistered and burned. She felt her muscles twitch as pain travelled along her left arm and through her body. Her heart pounded, then fluttered and faltered. Numbness began to spread along her limbs.

Christine felt oddly disconnected from her body. She could see her hand, her arm extended. She could feel the pain and ever-growing numbness. But it was as if she were experiencing the whole thing from a distance. Something is wrong, she realized. But what?

A customer in the shop ran over. "Are you all right?" he asked.

Christine heard his voice, but it sounded muffled and thick, as if she were wrapped in heavy gauze. She was having trouble hearing.

Suddenly the seriousness of the situation dawned on her. She snapped out of her trance. "I was hit by lightning," she cried. Her voice quivered, sounding thin and strained, as if it, too, had been damaged. "I was hit by lightning," she said again and again. Somehow repeating it made it seem more real.

Other workers in the shop came running. One person grabbed the phone, and stabbed at the buttons to call 911, but soon gave up. The lines were dead. Lightning had blown out the phone system.

Everyone huddled around Christine, anxious to help, uncertain just what to do. Christine tried walking, but her legs crumpled under her. Her left side was paralyzed, her breathing shallow. Her face lost its usual colour and slowly turned blue. Then, all at once, her breathing stopped. One moment

Christine was drawing air. The next she wasn't.

In her foggy state, she knew something was dangerously wrong. She was conscious, feeling her lungs fail, watching herself slowly strangle, but she was powerless to do anything about it. Breathe, she told herself. Come on, Christine — inhale. She suddenly gasped and drew a deep breath.

But Christine wasn't out of danger yet. A few minutes later her breathing stopped again. Start. Stop. Over and over. Christine wondered if one of those times her breathing would stop altogether.

Finally, her boss led her to a car and rushed her to the hospital. She received immediate attention. After an hour, her condition stabilized.

Now, years after the event, the effects of the lightning strike still linger. Christine tires easily. She talks slowly, cautiously, as if struggling to recall words. She has trouble hanging on to ideas. Memories and details come and go like drifting smoke. It's as if her brain has been scrambled, its circuitry mysteriously rewired. Sometimes her eyes play tricks on her, and her hearing has never been quite the same. Sounds clash and overlap. Even a simple conversation can seem like a symphony of noise.

"My life's changed," Christine says. "I can't do many of the things I once could." She has been forced to quit her job as an auto-body mechanic, a job she was once good at and loved. But, as different as her life has become, Christine Fram knows that she is one of the lucky ones. Lightning strikes more than 60 Canadians each year, and Christine is one of a handful of survivors. Her experience has left her with a deep respect for the forces of nature, and a strong yearning to help others. Since her accident, she has started a website devoted to lightning and its survivors.

Lightning Safety

• Being outdoors is dangerous during any lightning storm. Use the 30–30 rule to determine if you should seek shelter: Count the time between the lightning and thunder. If the time is thirty seconds or less, head for shelter immediately. Wait thirty minutes or more after hearing the last thunder before heading outdoors again.

• Do not take shelter under a tree. Avoid high places, open fields, and ridges above the tree line. If possible, go into a house or other sturdy building.

• If you are outdoors in an open area, kneel with your hands on the ground and your head low. Do NOT lie flat. This "lightning crouch" is safer than lying flat on the ground, because lying flat increases the chance of being hit by a current if lightning strikes the ground nearby.

• During the lightning storm, stay off corded telephones and away from any electrical appliances, lighting and sockets. Avoid contact with plumbing. If lightning strikes the building, it can travel along any of these conductors.

• Do not watch lightning from windows, doorways or porches. The safest place is in a room that does not have windows.

TIPS FOR SURVIVAL

131

OUT OF CONTROL

Nancy Kozlovic struggled with the controls, trying to pull the plane out of its spin. But it was too late. The plane veered sharply, and headed straight for a house.

From her seat at the controls of her small plane, Nancy Kozlovic could see the runway. She was skimming above it now, guiding the Cessna 150 two-seater toward a landing at the small airport just outside Guelph, Ontario. Another few seconds and she would be taxiing down the pavement, another solo flight successfully completed.

Landing an airplane is the trickiest part of flying, Nancy knew. There are so many things to consider — speed, angle, distance, altitude. But the forty-five-year-old pilot had more than seventy hours of flying experience, and she felt confident in her abilities. Besides, June 24, 1998, was a glorious day — hardly a cloud in the sky, scarcely a breeze — a perfect day for flying.

As the grey pavement zipped by, Nancy could see the end of the runway approaching. It was closer than she had first thought, and she knew instinctively that she had overshot the mark. She would have to abandon the landing and try another.

Nancy raised the wing flaps, and the plane began to bank to the right. But its nose was too high, the air speed too low. The plane began to lose altitude. Nancy struggled with the controls, trying to pull the plane out of its spin. But it was too late. The plane veered sharply and headed straight for a house near the airport.

The plane plunged 15 metres in seconds, hitting the ground with tremendous force, wheels bouncing over the lawn, propeller tearing through the air. The plane skimmed over the grass. Finally, the left wing clipped a spruce tree in the front yard, and the plane came to a jolting stop a few metres from the house.

Nancy Kozlovic's plane crashed right into a residential area

Nancy was shaken, but mostly relieved. It was a close call, as close as any she ever cared to have. She tugged at her seat belt, anxious now to get out of the broken plane. But the plane was leaning to the left, its wing wedged against the tree. With her weight pressing on the seat belt, it wouldn't open.

From the corner of her eye, Nancy caught sight of a glimmer of orange from the front of the plane. Fire! The engine was on fire! Nancy pulled harder, fumbling with the latch holding the belt closed. I have to get out, a voice inside her said. But the belt wouldn't budge. She was trapped.

Nancy could see flames flickering around the engine. Inside the cramped cockpit, temperatures soared. In a few moments the fire would spread to the cockpit and it, too, would erupt into flames with Nancy still trapped inside. "It happened so fast," Nancy said. "I knew I had thirty seconds left if I was lucky."

Above her rising panic, Nancy heard a sound. Someone was opening the door. Then, a man, James Munro, was by her side. He had been in a taxi on his way from the airport when he spotted Nancy's doomed plane drop to the ground.

133

The mangled plane, with scorch marks on the wing

James pulled on the seat belt, yanking with all his might. The latch wouldn't give.

"I can't get her out," Nancy heard James say. Then she realized that there was a second man by his side. Gerard Jansen had been working in the house Nancy's plane had nearly plowed into. He had been wallpapering the living room when he heard the thud of the plane hitting the ground. He ran from the house, discovered the plane, then ran back inside to call 911. By the time he came out again, fire was shooting high into the air, the tree in flames. Gerard was a farmer, accustomed to heavy work, but he couldn't get the seat-belt latch open either.

"Help!" Nancy pleaded, as flames enveloped the cockpit, setting her clothes and hair on fire. "Help me!"

There was no time to waste. Gerard grabbed Nancy. With one foot on the fuselage, he gave a mighty tug and lifted Nancy, slipping her through the still-locked belt loop and out of the plane. Behind them, the plane burst into flames.

Nancy could feel fire eating her clothes and licking her skin. James and Gerard patted the flames, trying to smother them with their hands. Stop, drop and roll, Nancy heard in her mind. She fell to the ground, rolling over and over until the fire was out.

Pain shot up her arms and legs. Her face felt blistered and raw. "Can you walk?" Gerard asked. Nancy nodded. Escorted by the men, she limped to the taxi James had jumped out of, and was taken to the local hospital. From there, she was shuttled by ambulance to the burn unit in nearby Hamilton, Ontario.

Gerard Jansen was honoured for his heroic act, receiving recognition from both the Carnegie Foundation and the Ontario Provincial Police.

Nancy, though, was severely injured. Second- and third-degree burns covered her legs, left arm, face and head. She spent five weeks in the hospital burn unit, receiving extensive skin grafts to heal her wounds. Infections slowed her recovery, and over the course of many months she endured painful rounds of physical therapy.

Despite her injuries, Nancy's spirit remained unbroken. Six weeks after the accident she was back at the Guelph airport sitting in a small plane, gathering the courage to fly again. Two weeks after that, she was in the air, a passenger in another plane. And soon she was flying herself. Within a year she obtained her private flying licence, and by May of 2001 she had earned both her commercial and instructor licences. Since then she has maintained an active lifestyle, hiking, dog sledding, setting new challenges and living life to the fullest.

The fire left Nancy's left leg damaged, and bearing numerous scars. She wears special leggings to ease the pain. Her face was also burned and, although it has healed somewhat, it still looks patchy and raw in places.

For a long time Nancy wore a facemask to speed up the healing, but now she is resigned to her new look. When she stares in a mirror, Nancy Kozlovic sees beyond the scars. She sees a different person than the one who looked back at her before the accident — a woman who is determined, persistent, strengthened by hardship. She hopes others will be able to see that, too.

FROM THE BRINK OF DEATH

By the time Kim Laverty reached the creek it was already too late. She could see little Sean McCarthy's blond hair in the river as his body bobbed to the surface and the rushing waters carried him away.

Kim Laverty dropped everything and ran. She tore across the yard and, in a few giant strides, was at the back gate. It was open and little Sean was nowhere to be seen. Beyond the yard lay Indian Head Creek. Kim scooted over to the bank, then froze in terror, her worst fears realized. She could see Sean's blond hair in the river, as his tiny body bobbed to the surface and the rushing water carried him away.

A few minutes earlier that Tuesday — April 10, 2001 — Sean McCarthy, a twenty-month-old toddler, had been in Kim's backyard in Hammond, Ontario, happily playing with the other children Kim baby-sat.

Kim had been keeping a watchful eye from her kitchen window while tending a sick child inside. A fence ringed the yard, protecting the children from the dangerous waters of the creek, only a stone's throw away. But, as sometimes happens in spite of all precautions, fate stepped in to change things. Kim's dog, who was sharing the yard with Sean, nudged open the back gate. In no time, the little boy was over the bank and in the water.

Kim watched helplessly as Sean was swept away. She ran alongside the creek, stumbling over stones, wading into the icy water, trying to grab him. But he was out of reach, and often out of sight. Kim spotted him now and then as he rose to the surface, but each time he disappeared again, sucked under the water by the swift current.

At one point Sean was swept through a culvert under a road. He vanished, then seconds later appeared on the other side. Kim crossed the road, then stopped. The other children had followed her and were dangerously close to the swirling creek. She had no choice. Kim turned around, children in tow, and rushed home. Quickly she dialled 911.

———

Patrick Guindon, a volunteer fireman, was having lunch at home a block away. When the emergency call came through on his pager, he headed to Kim's address. Kim found someone to supervise the children, and within minutes the two adults were scouring the bank. They spotted Kim's dog as it followed Sean. For more than half a kilometre Kim and Patrick raced beside the rushing water, keeping their eyes on Sean, who was being carried face down in the swiftly moving creek. Once in a while Sean floated close to the bank, almost close enough to touch, to grab, to hold tight. But each time they drew near, the current picked him up and carried him away.

Then a small miracle happened. An overhanging branch snagged Sean's coat as he drifted past. For a moment, he was caught. Patrick dove into the water, swam 10 metres and unhooked Sean. With Kim's help, he carried the toddler to shore.

Sean was lifeless, his lips an eerie blue, his body as cold as ice. Patrick felt for a pulse, but found none. Sean had been in the creek for at least ten minutes. Most people can survive two or three — maybe even four — minutes underwater. After that the body shuts down. The heart stops, and bit by bit the brain switches off and dies. Immediately Patrick started CPR. He applied pressure to Sean's chest and forced air into his lungs. He got no response. Still, Patrick kept trying.

He was still at it when a helicopter landed. As luck would have it, an air ambulance happened to be close by when the emergency call went through. Paramedics took over. They scooped up Sean and rushed him to the intensive care unit of a nearby hospital.

Sean was ice-cold. After being in the frigid waters for so long, his body temperature was 26°C, eleven degrees below normal. There were no vital signs — not a single tiny breath from the frail body, not a single heartbeat. Technically, the toddler was dead. But doctors knew that extreme cold does

Sean McCarthy after the accident

strange things to the human body. By lowering Sean's body temperature and slowing down his metabolism, the cold might have actually protected him. If his temperature could be raised, and if his heart could be started again, there was still a chance that Sean could be brought back from death.

Doctors and nurses sprang into action. Warm fluids were forced into Sean's body to raise its temperature. He was hooked up to a heart-and-lung bypass machine to circulate his blood. All the while, resuscitation efforts continued. For two and a half hours hospital staff worked feverishly. All that time there were no detectable signs of life in Sean's small body. Then, there it was — a pulse, a glimmer of a heartbeat, a shred of hope that Sean might make a complete recovery.

Sean was placed on a ventilator to help his breathing. He was kept heavily sedated to give his body a chance to return to normal. After forty-eight hours, doctors reported that there was no evidence of damage to Sean's major organs. It was the first hurdle in the long road to recovery, and everyone breathed a sign of relief. But Sean was still in a coma and there were nagging questions that needed to be answered. When would he awaken? When he did, would he still be the bright, blue-eyed boy with the easy smile and winning ways? Or would his oxygen-starved brain be somehow altered forever?

On Saturday morning, a full four days after the accident, Sean awoke. He reached over, grabbed his favourite toy — a stuffed monkey — clutched it to his chest and went back to sleep. It was a small act, but a significant one. It was a sign that the same Sean was about to return.

Since that time, Sean has made a full recovery, a fact that is miraculous.

━━━

"We think *what if* a lot," his mother, Natalie, said. What if the branch had not snagged Sean? What if Patrick had not picked up the call, or had been more than a block away? What if the helicopter had not been nearby? What if . . .?

But some things cannot be explained, and Natalie McCarthy knows that she has much to be grateful for. "The little things mean more than they used to. Life is precious."

Surviving Hypothermia

Hypothermia is caused by prolonged exposure to cold. As the inner core of the body cools, the victim shivers uncontrollably, becomes uncoordinated, and has difficulty speaking and thinking clearly. Pulse and respiration slow and, unless help is given quickly, the victim can lapse into unconsciousness and even die. Here's what to do at the first signs of hypothermia:

TIPS FOR SURVIVAL

• Seek shelter from the rain and cold.

• Get out of the wind. Even a slight breeze carries body heat away at an alarming rate. If you cannot find shelter, wrap plastic bags, tarps or other wind-proof materials around your body.

• Remove wet clothes. Get into a sleeping bag or dry warm clothing.

• Drink warm fluids. Eat high-energy foods such as fruit and candy.

• Share body heat with a partner.

• Resist sleep. There is a danger of lapsing into unconsciousness if body temperatures drop further.

IMMENSE COURAGE

With his leg pinned under a boulder, Bill Jeracki knew he'd never survive the night. When his fingers curled around the knife in his pocket, he knew what he had to do.

Every time Bill Jeracki moved, each time he shifted position or tried to free his leg, pain shot through his body. Bill was trapped, and had been for hours. He was alone on a deserted mountain, his mangled left leg wedged beneath a boulder. No one knew his whereabouts. No one knew he was missing.

Bill Jeracki had come to the St. Mary's Glacier region of western Colorado to fish. That October morning in 1993 he had trekked up a winding mountain trail. Somewhere along the route his foot caught on loose stone and Bill slipped off the trail, skidding a few metres down the slope and landing on his back with a thud. His fall dislodged a boulder. It tumbled downhill, coming to a crushing halt on top of Bill's lower leg.

Bill tried pushing the boulder aside, but it was too heavy. He tried wiggling himself free, but each twist or turn just made things worse. After a few hours of trying, he was exhausted. His hopes, like his leg, were crushed. There seemed to be no way of freeing himself, and no possibility of rescue.

The afternoon was slipping away quickly. In a few hours darkness would cover the mountain. A storm was brewing, too. Weather is fickle in the high regions of the Rocky Mountains, and even in early summer, snowstorms are commonplace. Dressed in a light vest and flannel shirt, Bill feared he would never survive the night. Either the cold would kill him or he would die from his injuries.

Unless . . . Bill's fingers curled around the knife in his pocket. Unless . . . But the thought was too horrifying, too repulsive — there had to be another way. But the more he thought about it, the more Bill realized that it was his only option. To survive, he needed to cut off his own leg.

140

Bill took the knife out of his pocket, opened the blade, stared at the gleaming metal . . . and hesitated. He worked as an anaesthetist in a hospital and had attended many surgeries. He knew a thing or two about the human body. The tissue around the kneecap was soft. The bones connecting the upper and lower legs were held together with sinew and ligaments. With just the right cut, they would sever easily. It would take courage, though, immense courage and a strength that Bill wasn't sure he possessed.

"It took a great deal of time to psych myself into laying a sharp edge to my skin," Bill said later. He thought about his wife, Kate, and remembered saying goodbye to her that morning. Bill thought about their children, too. They deserved a father to watch over them, to be part of their lives; that much he owed them. Better a father with only one leg than no father at all.

Finally Bill tore off his flannel shirt and tied it to his leg just above the knee. Using a nearby oak branch, he twisted the shirt tight, making a tourniquet to apply pressure to slow down the bleeding. Then, holding his breath and bracing himself against the pain, he made the first cut. The knife slid effortlessly into the soft tissue under the kneecap. Bill sliced and sawed, slowly cutting away the flesh that held his leg together.

More than once, Bill had to stop. "It was the most horrible thing that I've ever been through. I would take some slashing cuts, and then have to back off and catch my breath."

But each time Bill forced himself back to the gruesome task. The worst moment came as the blade severed the nerve that ran behind the knee. Bill clenched his teeth and fought a wave of nausea. He thought for sure he would pass out from the pain.

Then it was over. The knife sliced through the last shreds of flesh, and he was free. But there was no time to waste. Bill knew he needed to find help fast. The tourniquet was just temporary. Without immediate medical attention, he would bleed to death in the mountains.

Bill lay on his back, and using his arms like paddles, pushed himself down the slope. It was a slow process. After what seemed like an eternity, he reached the trailhead where he had parked his truck earlier that day. He hobbled toward it and dragged himself into the driver's seat. It was a relief to hear the engine start, but Bill realized that he faced a new challenge — driving the truck down the winding mountain road with only one foot.

Bill ground the truck into gear, then swiftly moved his right foot to the gas pedal to get the truck moving. Alternating between brake and gas pedals, he manoeuvred the truck down the curving road. Around each turn, he fought to stay alert, to remain conscious.

Eventually, he reached a small village. Someone called 911. Paramedics arrived and Bill was swiftly airlifted to a near-by hospital, where he was rushed into surgery. Meanwhile, hikers trekked back into the mountains to retrieve the leg that was still wedged under the boulder. They brought it to the hospital. Unfortunately, it was too badly damaged to reattach.

Months of therapy followed. Bill was fitted with a prosthetic leg and he quickly recovered, but the experience profoundly changed his life. He learned to cherish each moment with his family. He also gave up one career to begin another — fitting prosthetics on other amputees.

Would Bill have survived the night on the mountain if he hadn't taken such drastic measures? Bill is convinced that he made the right choice. The night of the accident, temperatures plunged and a snowstorm swept the mountain, dumping 16 centimetres of snow on its windswept slopes.

As far as Bill Jeracki is concerned, a leg was a small price to pay to save his own life. "I did it to get off that mountain. I said [I'd] accept whatever comes. That's all you can do in that situation."

Controlling Bleeding

Bill Jeracki saved his own life by using a tourniquet to stop the flow of blood. Tourniquets, however, are a last, desperate measure. Left too long, a tourniquet can starve the limbs of blood, leading to gangrene and other complications. For most ordinary cuts, use other means of pressure to stop the bleeding:

TIPS FOR SURVIVAL

• For minor bleeding, elevate the injury. Apply a bandage or clean cloth to the cut and hold it firmly in place until clotting occurs and blood flow stops.

• For more severe bleeding, elevate the injury and put pressure directly on the wound by covering it with sterile pads, clothes — even your hand. Hold for ten minutes. Apply another pad or cloth over the blood-soaked one if bleeding continues.

• If bleeding continues, apply pressure to the closest pressure point to the wound. Pressure points lie near the skin's surface where large arteries that supply blood to the arms and legs are. By pressing the artery at the pressure point against the bone directly behind it, you can control the flow of blood. The most common pressure points are located in the upper arms between the armpit and elbow, and in the creases on the insides of the upper legs near the crotch.

FAITHFUL FRIEND

Jim Tarpley lay in the dirt under the blazing sun, too broken and battered to move. Whether he lived or died depended on Leroy, his faithful dog.

Jim Tarpley speaks with a slight drawl, his gravelly voice lingering between words as if he is giving them special consideration. It's just what you would expect from a rugged cattle rancher who has weathered a lot of storms over the years. But when Jim speaks of Leroy, his voice mellows and there's a hint of emotion in it. Leroy is the reason that Jim is alive today.

Leroy was Jim's dog. The Airedale was, in Jim's words, "a sorry looking animal." With long delicate legs that seemed to lose themselves in thick brown fur, the gangly dog looked out of place on the ranch. But what Leroy lacked in looks, he made up for in spirit.

Wherever Jim travelled, Leroy was never far behind. The dog shadowed his master, keeping Jim company as he did his chores around the ranch in eastern Idaho. But life for the pair was more than just work. There was time for games and relaxation, too.

One of their favourite games was "let's go irrigate." Whenever Jim checked the ranch's irrigation system, Leroy followed closely, knowing that at any moment Jim might stop and say, "All right, Leroy, let's go irrigate!" The words sent shivers of excitement through Leroy's shaggy body. Like a loosed arrow, he would race to the ditch and plunge into the water for a refreshing dip.

At sunrise on the morning of July 16, 1988, Jim and Leroy set out in the truck to make their rounds of the ranch. The sky was a brilliant blue, and the day promised to be a scorcher. They bounced for several kilometres down a dirt road before stopping in a meadow to load bales of hay. Jim fired up a big

Leroy

diesel tractor, scooped up the bales and piled them on a wagon. When he had a full load he carted the wagon across the field and stacked the bales into neat rows.

Around 8:30 a.m. a gear on the bale wagon jammed. Jim started to climb down from the tractor to free it. His foot slipped on a blob of grease and he grabbed a control bar on the tractor to steady himself. The tractor swung into gear and lurched ahead, throwing Jim to the ground. On his way down, he accidentally hit the throttle. The tractor roared to life. Its giant wheels rolled forward, crushing Jim. He felt his leg shatter. Then, as the tractor rumbled over his chest, he felt his ribs crack and splinter.

The wheels narrowly missed Jim's head as the tractor chugged past and headed across the field. Jim lay on his back, crumpled and broken. Any movement, no matter how slight, sent waves of pain through his body. He knew he was critically injured, that time was important to his survival. But he couldn't move. He could hardly breathe.

Jim heard the cough of an engine and felt the ground

quiver. The tractor sounded too close. Unable to raise his head because of his injuries, Jim grabbed his hair with his hand and lifted his head up so he could look. Somehow the tractor had bounced off some bales, and turned around in a tight circle. It was grinding its way back, and Jim was right in its path.

Fighting the pain, Jim twisted his mangled body and rolled over three times. The tractor roared past, just missing him. Then, the incredible happened. One of the wheels hit an oil can. The tractor twisted, turned and circled back. This time there was no escape. The wheels bounced over Jim's legs, crushing them once again.

The tractor's steering was locked, and it was moving in an endless circle. In a few seconds, Jim knew, it would swing back and run over him again. This is it . . . the end, Jim told himself. He prepared for the final crunch and prayed for a quick death.

Then the incredible happened once again. As the tractor chugged by the truck, the bale wagon snagged it. The tractor shifted directions, rumbled past Jim, climbed a small hill, and stalled near a barbed-wire fence. With the tractor engine dead, an eerie stillness filled the air. Jim dared not move, could not move. He lay face down in the dirt, his body shattered, his insides pulverized.

Leroy wandered over and licked Jim's face. "I'm still alive," Jim whispered, hardly believing it himself. The morning wore on. The sun rose higher in the sky, leaving no escape from the blazing heat. Jim drifted in and out of consciousness. Sometimes, when he awoke, Leroy was there lying beside him. Other times the dog was gone.

By one o'clock Jim's mouth was papery dry and his tongue was swollen and thick. He tried to whistle for Leroy, but no sound came from his lips. Blowflies circled around him and crawled into his nose, ears and eyes. Jim was too weak to shoo them away. He had stopped sweating, too, a sure sign that he was becoming dangerously dehydrated.

Leroy wandered over. He had been swimming in the ditch, and water dripped from his thick coat. He plopped down in the dirt next to Jim and licked him, working his tongue over Jim's wounds and chasing away the blowflies that peppered his face. The coolness of Leroy's wet fur revived Jim. He began sucking on Leroy's coat, drawing as much moisture as he could. The water trickled down his throat and soaked into its parched lining. It felt good, so good. But Jim knew he needed more if he was to survive.

"Leroy," he whispered. "Let's go irrigate."

Leroy bounded to the nearby creek, then he returned, dripping wet. Jim sucked as much water as he could, then sent Leroy to "go irrigate" again and again.

The afternoon dragged on unmercifully. Jim knew he was a mangled mess, and that if he didn't receive help before nightfall he wouldn't live to see the next day. Thoughts of his family crossed his mind. He saw the faces of his wife and their four grown children. There are so many things I want to tell them, he thought. He stretched out his unbroken arm and scratched *I love . . .* in the dirt. But he couldn't finish. He didn't have the strength.

Around 4:00 o'clock Jim heard the sound of a car tearing down the dirt road. He grabbed his straw hat, raised his arm and waved. Please see me, he begged.

The car screeched to a stop and two of Jim's neighbours tumbled out.

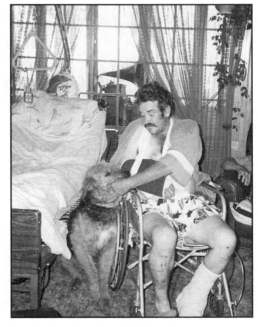

Jim Tarpley at home, recovering from the accident, with Leroy at his side

147

Jim's memories of the next few hours are hazy, and broken by long stretches of uncosciousness. He remembers a medevac helicopter arriving. He recalls the ride to the hospital, the shots and intravenous drips along the way. He remembers snippets of conversations on the helicopter, the whispered gasp of a nurse saying, "I can't find a pulse." He remembers hearing the doctor telling the pilot, "We're going to lose him if you don't get there faster."

It took twenty-six minutes to reach the hospital. In that time, Jim hovered between life and death. Doctors said his chances were slim, that he would likely not survive the night. They ushered in his wife and children to say their goodbyes.

Jim surprised them all. He pulled through, despite his punctured bladder, shattered pelvis, crushed ribs and fractured leg, arm, hand and shoulder. After thirteen days in the hospital, he was sent home encased in casts and bandages, to face months of painful therapy.

Jim credits Leroy with saving his life. "That dog," he says, "was special. He would do anything for me." So special was the dog that, when Leroy died in 1992, it just seemed natural for Jim to bury him on the ranch. So special that, when Jim finally sold the ranch, he dug up the dog's remains and reburied him near his new home in the mountains of Idaho. Leroy would like the new place, Jim figured. It seemed to be the least he could do for his friend.

EPILOGUE
You, the Survivor

Why do some people survive while others do not?

No doubt luck plays a part in survival. Many survivors in this book owe their lives to eerie twists of fate and events beyond their own control. Angela Paulson would likely have frozen to death if the telephone hadn't rung when it did. Young Ed Glanz happened to be at the right window during a terrible fire; other students in his classroom weren't so fortunate. Jeffrey Bush could have been seriously disfigured if he hadn't been wearing a wedding ring, and little Sean McCarthy owes his life in part to a tree branch in a swirling creek.

Often, though, there's more than luck involved. Herbert Nishimoto didn't wait for luck to intervene — he fashioned a rickety raft out of debris around him, and saved his own life. Jim Tarpley saw opportunity in a dripping dog. Chris Duddy fought poisonous fumes and slippery slopes to climb out of a volcano. Andy Carter took advantage of a freak twist of his surfboard.

Resourcefulness, swift action, courage, determination — all of these mix and merge in unpredictable ways. When it comes to survival, there is no simple formula to follow. Each survivor's story is as individual as the person involved, as unique as its own circumstances.

Still, there are things we can learn from survivors. There are things we can do to increase our own chances if danger arises.

Be Informed

Knowing what to do in difficult situations has helped many survivors to beat the odds. Patrick Hedges understood fires and used his knowledge to lead his family to safety in a firestorm. Bill Jeracki knew first aid and a thing or two about the human body. Anhydrous ammonia was no stranger to Lee Wieland. He understood its dangers, and used that information to help his family stay alive.

By being familiar with danger and knowing how to react, we strengthen our chances of surviving. Reading about survival experiences is a start. Taking note of survival tips such as those in this book is another. Safety and survival courses also provide essential information.

Before venturing into a cave, take a course in caving. Before heading into the forest, take a wilderness survival class or stop at a ranger station to obtain information. Study emergency first aid — who knows when that will be useful? Do whatever you can to understand danger and how to handle it.

Plan for the Worst

No one knows exactly when disaster might strike, but being prepared for the worst in each situation gives us an edge. Even though Matt Sanders expected to be back in a day, he took food, a sleeping bag and other supplies on his hike. That foresight helped him to survive six days in a blizzard. Tony Bullimore's yacht was equipped with survival gear, allowing him to endure several days in his capsized yacht. Ken Rutland carried extra clothing in his backpack, an action that helped him to save the lives of two men on an avalanche-swept mountain.

Anticipate danger and plan for it. Take note of exits in buildings. Plan an escape route from your home. Plot an evacuation route from your neighbourhood. Store emergency equipment nearby, and check periodically to see that it is in tip-top condition. Leave blankets, candles and a shovel in the car in winter. Check weather conditions before heading outdoors. Take along extra food and clothing on hikes. Carry a cell phone, two-way radio or walkie-talkie, so you can call for help if you need it. Think of the danger ahead and prepare for it.

Stay Calm

Among survivors, cool heads prevailed. "The best advice I can give is to stay calm," said survivor Ed Glanz. "Force yourself to think clearly."

Caught in life-and-death situations, many survivors kept their wits about them and reacted calmly despite their rising fear. Knowing that panic would only cause him to sink faster into quicksand, Terry Howlett willed himself to be still. Despite his severe injuries from a grizzly attack, Bram Schaffer calmly plotted an escape route through the forest. Even with her clothes on fire, Nancy Kozlovic squelched her fear and remembered to stop, drop and roll.

Some survivors found peace through their beliefs. Gustavo Badillo drew comfort from prayer while he was trapped in an underwater cave. So did the Wieland family as they huddled in a chilly attic, trying to escape poisonous fumes, and the Hedges huddling in a stream as they outwaited a fiery inferno.

Nothing clouds the mind and paralyses the body like unbridled fear. As difficult as it might be, pushing aside fear and reacting with calm reason may be your best defence against danger.

Give Yourself Reasons to Live

With his leg trapped under a boulder, Bill Jeracki thought of his family. They needed him, and that thought kept him going even though his situation looked desperate. A battered and broken Jim Tarpley did the same.

These survivors, like many others, convinced themselves that they needed to survive. When confronting danger and impossible situations, give yourself reasons to survive. Set goals. Visualize family and friends. Talk yourself into living.

Don't Give Up

Persistence and determination go a long way in survival. Despite the constant threat of avalanches, Ken Rutland would not abandon the two men he found trapped in the snow. Even though they were seriously wounded in animal attacks, Val Plumwood, Bram Schaffer and Andy Carter all dragged themselves to safety. What else but tremendous tenacity can explain how Joe Spring managed to stay alive for so long in his crumpled car? Would Ed Glanz be alive today if he hadn't held on to the fireman, refusing to let go?

Faced with unbeatable odds, injury — even death — many survivors simply refused to give up. They fought all the way, with all of their strength and will. Do the same and you, too, may be a survivor if danger calls.

The publisher thanks the following for supplying photographs:

Pages 4 and 5, NOAA

Page 11, Hawaii Volcanoes National Park via SODA

Page 15, Federal Emergency Management Agency, FEMA

Pages 19 and 22, Pacific Tsunami Museum

Page 20, NOAA

Page 27, Richard Armstrong, courtesy of National Snow and Ice Data Center

Page 28, courtesy of Ken Rutland

Page 29, Office of the Governor General/Government of Canada

Page 33, Adrian Wyld/CP Archives, CP CGY104

Page 36, Corel (Predators)

Page 39, courtesy of Jim and Wendy White

Page 44, courtesy of Mike Pingleton

Page 50, Southwest News Service

Page 53, Corel (Predators)

Page 59, Themba Hadebe/Associated Press, 0U1W5

Page 61, Karel Prisloo/Associated Press, 0U566

Page 65, courtesy of Angela Paulson

Page 69, Hawaii Volcanoes National Park via SODA

Page 76, courtesy of Therese Wallin

Page 82, Bill Hatto/Associated Press, 056VA

Pages 87 and 88, courtesy of the family of Joe Spring

Page 91, Photodisc via SODA

Pages 98 and 100, Chicago Historical Society

Pages 108 and 109, Lancaster and Morecambe Newspapers

Page 113, courtesy of the Wieland family

Pages 118 and 121, Michael Reiger, Federal Emergency Management Agency, FEMA

Page 122, courtesy of Guide Dogs for the Blind

Page 129, NOAA

Pages 133, courtesy of the Transportation Safety Board of Canada, reproduced with the permission of the Minister of Public Works and Government Services Canada, 2002.

Page 138, courtesy of Natalie McCarthy

Pages 145 and 147, courtesy of Jim Tarpley